COUNTRY LIVING

ONE-DISH
COUNTRY SUPPERS

COUNTRY LIVING

ONE-DISH COUNTRY SUPPERS

Delicious Casseroles, Fritattas, Roasts, and Stews

HEARST BOOKS

A division of Sterling Publishing Co., Inc.

New York / London
www.sterlingpublishing.com

Supplemental text by Kathleen Hackett
Book and cover design by Gretchen Scoble Design

Library of Congress Cataloging-in-Publication Data
Country living one-dish country suppers : delicious casseroles, fritattas, roasts, and stews / from the editors of Country living magazine.
    p. cm.
Includes index.
ISBN 978-1-58816-718-7
1. One-dish meals. 2. Suppers. I. Country living (New York, N.Y.) II. Title: One-dish country suppers.
TX840.O53C68 2008
641.8'2--dc22
                          2008011843

10 9 8 7 6 5 4 3 2 1

Published by Hearst Books
A Division of Sterling Publishing Co., Inc.
387 Park Avenue South, New York, NY 10016

Country Living and Hearst Books are trademarks of Hearst Communications, Inc.

www.countryliving.com

For information about custom editions, special sales, premium and corporate purchases, please contact Sterling Special Sales Department at 800-805-5489 or specialsales@sterlingpublishing.com.

Distributed in Canada by Sterling Publishing
c/o Canadian Manda Group, 165 Dufferin Street
Toronto, Ontario, Canada M6K 3H6

Distributed in Australia by Capricorn Link (Australia) Pty. Ltd.
P.O. Box 704, Windsor, NSW 2756 Australia

Manufactured in China

Sterling ISBN 978-1-58816-718-7

Contents

Foreword

Through my travels for the magazine—and for pleasure—I have dined at some of the finest restaurants around the country and have had equally memorable meals at out-of-the-way seafood shacks, barbecue pits, and county fairs. But as much as I enjoy eating out, I do love cooking at home, whether it's a simple weekday supper or a more formal or larger gathering with family and friends. Like many of you, I am drawn to comfort foods: recipes that are nutritious, fresh, familiar, and wholesome. I also look for meals that are time-efficient, easy to prepare, serve, and clean up. That's why this book, *One-Dish Country Suppers* was such a pleasure to create.

On the following pages, you will find some of our favorite "one-dish" recipes from the pages of *Country Living* magazine. And if you think that one-dish meals can't be special, this book will certainly change your perceptions. There are recipes that require very little effort and bring such deeply satisfying results that you will want to make them again and again. There are recipes for every taste and every occasion, from Coq au Vin Blanc to Potato and Onion Tart to Indian-Spiced Lamb Chili. While the recipes vary in terms of prep and cook times, all are easy, nutritious, and delicious. The fact that they are cooked in a Dutch oven (one of my favorite ways to cook), skillet, or slow cooker is an added bonus, since they can go straight from the oven to the table and, as such, require less time for cleanup. I know you will want to try many of the recipes in this book. I am certain that more than a few will become your new favorites!

—Nancy Mernit Soriano
Editor in Chief, Country Living

Introduction

If you think back on some of your most memorable meals, chances are you didn't eat them in a fancy restaurant or at formal dinner parties. It's more likely that dinner was a simple yet delicious offering—a soup, stew, roast, or braise—that a friend put together with no fancy tools, techniques, or exotic ingredients. Tempting aromas filled the air, and when it was time to sit down at the table, dinner appeared effortlessly, perhaps served up in a humble cast iron pan, a colorful enameled cast iron pot, or a handsome skillet. *Country Living One-Dish Country Suppers* is a collection of recipes for dishes just like that—deliciously simple and classic one-pot comfort foods that are just as perfect for weekday meals as they are for easy entertaining.

On the following pages, you will find many traditional one-pot recipes—beef stew, pot pie, chili, chicken noodle soup among them—that are perfect for feeding your family and friends. And while such familiar one-dish standards as lasagna, chowder, and hash are here, there are many other recipes included that might surprise you. Salmon and Goat Cheese Frittata (page 97), Spinach and Cheese Pie (page 107) and Onion and Potato Tart (page 53), for example, all fall into *Country Living's* definition of one-dish suppers, too; they're all easy to prepare, delicious, nutritious, and don't involve special equipment to prepare.

The beauty of one-dish cooking lies in the ease with which you can put a home-cooked dinner on the table whatever the occasion. Indeed, in most cases, all that's needed to round out the menu is a lightly dressed green salad and perhaps a baguette picked up on the way home from work. But there are other advantages to recommend it as well. Whether dinner is in an hour—or in two or four—there's a one-dish recipe to suit a range of time frames. There are skillet-cooked dishes that can be prepared in 30 minutes as well as braises that slow-cook for several hours. Even still, these ask for little to no attention from the cook. Korean-Style Short Ribs, for example, cook for about $2\frac{1}{2}$ hours, but you only need to tend to them twice during that time. If you're in a hurry to get dinner on the table, creamy Gorgonzola-Buttermilk Pasta with Arugula can be ready in 30 minutes or less. The most compelling reason to make the recipes in this book part of your own repertoire, however, just might be because they taste great.

ONE-POT COOKING POTS AND PANS

In order to thoroughly enjoy and take advantage of one-dish cooking, you need only a few essential pieces of good basic cookware. A Dutch oven and a cast iron or stainless steel skillet are all that's really required. If you have a slow cooker, all the better.

CAST IRON

Cast iron is inexpensive and heats evenly and consistently. Even better, it lasts a lifetime if you take proper care of it. You can find cast-iron skillets for sale at cooking stores, thrift shops, flea markets, and tag sales. Don't turn away from those that are well-used; like red wine, cast iron pans improve with age. You can easily clean up and reseason one. Seasoning is simply "cooking" oil into the pores of the metal so that the surface is smooth and nonstick. If cast iron is properly seasoned, food will never stick to it and cleanup will be a snap. That said, there are several companies that manufacture pre-seasoned, maintenance-free cast iron pans.

If you purchase a cast iron skillet new, before you season it, you must first remove the protective food-safe wax that coats it by scrubbing the skillet with a stainless steel scouring pad, soap, and very hot water. To season a cast iron pan:

1. Wash the pan with dish washing liquid and hot water. Do not let the pan sit in soapy water for prolonged periods. Rinse and dry thoroughly. To insure that it is completely dry, place the pan on a hot burner for 2 to 3 minutes.

2. While the pan is hot and on the burner, carefully and lightly oil the inside surfaces with any vegetable or neutral oil.

3. Leave the pan on the burner for about 3 minutes. Remove and wipe out excess oil from the pan with a paper towel.

4. Store all cast iron cookware with the lids off to prevent moisture build up, which in turn, can cause rust. Never store cast iron without drying it thoroughly.

5. If your food begins to take on a metallic taste or is turning black, the problem can be one of two things: the pan isn't seasoned properly or there is food residue in the pan. This is especially true for acidic foods, which break down the pan's seasoning, causing them to acquire a metallic flavor. Avoid cooking acidic foods such as vinegar, tomatoes, and citrus in cast iron for this reason.

6. Never use detergent to wash cast iron unless you are planning to reseason it.

7. Avoid submerging a hot cast iron pan in cold water; it can crack.

8. In general, cast iron should be reseasoned every two years.

ENAMELED COOKWARE

If cast iron doesn't suit you, a good alternative is enamel-coated cast iron pots. This cookware, which features an off-white interior and is available in myriad colors, has a protective inner coating of enamel that doesn't allow flavors to be absorbed into the pot. Like cast iron, it conducts heat evenly and consistently. Unlike cast iron, an enamel pot can chip if you drop or bang it. If this happens, treat the bruise as you would cast iron: dry the area very well after each cleaning and rub a neutral oil into the exposed area. The white enamel lining of enamel pots can also stain. To return the interior of the pot to its original color, clean it with a paste made from baking soda and water. Alternatively, fill it with water, add a capful of bleach to the pot and let it sit overnight. Be sure to thoroughly wash it with dishwashing liquid before using. The only other downside to these imminently useful pots is the price. Compared to an uncoated cast iron pot, which might cost $25, a good enamel-coated Dutch oven, for example, can be as much as $200. With that price tag, however, comes a practical—and very handsome—pot that you will always be pleased to put on the dinner table.

HEAVY-BOTTOMED SKILLETS

A skillet is another great one-dish wonder tool. Heavy stainless steel pans with copper bottoms, hard anodized steel skillets, and those clad with aluminum sandwiched between stainless steel are among the most versatile pieces of kitchen equipment and one every kitchen should have. These skillets are meant to last a lifetime and, with the proper care, they will. Heavy-bottomed pans heat foods evenly and gently. To clean these skillets, use hot, soapy water; if you are trying to remove baked-on food, products designed specifically to clean stainless steel such as Cameo Stainless Steel Cleaner or Steel Brite will do the trick. To remove heat stains—they're typically golden brown or blue—use Barkeeper's Friend, a powdered cleanser that has multiple uses. All of these products can be found in some supermarkets and most kitchenware stores. Either way, you'll want to take care.

SLOW COOKERS

Slow cookers—crock pots—were once considered old-fashioned, but they enjoy renewed popularity today and understandably so. What could be more convenient than tossing a handful of ingredients into a pot in the morning, going about your daily routine, and arriving home to an aromatic, mouthwatering meal? Slow cookers are eminently foolproof to use, but there are a few things to keep in mind. Since temperatures must reach at least 165°F for safe slow cooking, be sure to use a model in which the lowest heat setting is 200°F. Always use fully thawed meat to prevent any possibility of it being under-cooked. Resist the urge to lift the lid of the cooker—you lose 15 to 20 minutes of cooking time every time you do! While tossing everything but the kitchen sink into a slow cooker is fine, more flavorful results are achieved if you prepare your ingredients a bit first. Brown meat and sauté vegetables before popping them in the pot and, to create a thick sauce, dredge the meat in flour before browning. Trim excess fat off meat when you combine it with vegetables to insure even cooking and layer the ingredients so that the vegetables are on the bottom and the meat sits on top. If you are going to add milk, butter, or cream to the pot, do so just before the cooking time is complete since dairy products tend to break down when exposed to excessive heat.

With the right equipment and the wonderful recipes on the following pages, preparing fantastic meals without fuss will make enjoying them that much better.

Beef, Veal, Lamb & Pork

The brown-lacquered sheen on these delectable ribs comes from a heady mix of dark beer, soy sauce, fresh-grated ginger, and chili paste. As the ribs simmer, their spicy braising liquid reduces down to a rich sauce that is delectable spooned over rice.

Korean-Style Short Ribs

3½ **pounds beef short ribs**

½ **teaspoon salt**

½ **teaspoon ground black pepper**

3 **tablespoons canola oil**

3 **cups low-sodium beef broth**

2 **cups water**

½ **cup medium-dark beer**

¼ **cup low-sodium soy sauce**

5 **large cloves garlic, sliced**

1 **tablespoon plus 1 teaspoon grated peeled fresh ginger**

2 **teaspoons chili or chili-garlic paste**

¼ **teaspoon ground dried chiles**

3 **medium carrots, peeled and cut into 2-inch chunks**

½ **pound onions (about 2 medium), cut into 1-inch wedges**

3 **green onions, sliced**

★ MAKE THE RIBS: Preheat oven to 350°F. Season the ribs with salt and pepper. In a Dutch oven, heat the oil over high heat until hot but not smoking. Sear the ribs until browned on all sides. Remove the ribs from the pan and discard the fat. When the pan has cooled slightly, add the beef broth, water, beer, soy sauce, garlic, ginger, chili paste, ground chiles, and the browned ribs. Bring to a boil over medium-high heat. Cover, transfer to the oven, and cook for 1 hour. Turn the ribs over and skim off any fat. Cover and cook for 1 more hour. Skim off any fat and add the carrots and onions. Cover and cook until the meat and vegetables are tender—about 30 more minutes. Garnish with the green onions and serve immediately.

Tip Serve with the same amber beer or ale you used to make the sauce. If wine is the preferred drink, offer a dark zinfandel or luxurious syrah.

NUTRITION INFORMATION PER SERVING—protein: 98.4 g; fat: 65.5 g; carbohydrate: 17 g; fiber: 2.8 g; sodium: 1,024 mg; cholesterol: 276 mg; calories: 1,079.

Three tiers of grilled steak, mild cheese, beans, and tomatoes, each separated by corn tortillas, comprise this company-worthy version of the taco. Serve it with sour cream and salsa on the side.

Tortilla Casserole

1 pound boneless beef sirloin steak

6 tablespoons fresh lime juice

1/2 teaspoon ground ancho chile pepper

1/4 teaspoon salt

2 ears fresh corn, husked and silked

1 large red onion, cut into 1/2-inch slices

2 tablespoons olive oil

1 15-ounce can black beans, rinsed
   and drained

1 15-ounce can kidney beans, rinsed
   and drained

2 jalapeño peppers, seeded and sliced
   into 1/8-inch rounds

1 teaspoon chopped chipotle pepper

1/4 cup low-sodium chicken broth or water

1/2 teaspoon grated lime zest

6 corn tortillas

2 cups shredded Monterey Jack cheese

4 tomatoes, cut into 1/4-inch slices

11/2 teaspoons chopped fresh
   oregano leaves

★ MARINATE THE STEAK: In a shallow glass dish, place the steak. Add 2 tablespoons of the lime juice, the ancho powder, and salt. Rub the ingredients into both sides of the steak; cover loosely and let marinate for 30 minutes.

★ GRILL THE STEAK AND VEGETABLES: Coat the corn and red onion slices with olive oil. On a medium-hot grill, place the steak, corn, and onion slices. Grill the steak until rare—about 5 minutes per side. Grill the corn, turning once or twice, until golden brown. Grill the onion slices, turning once, until tender. Remove all from the heat.

★ MAKE THE FILLING: Preheat oven to 400°F. Cut the grilled steak into 1/4-inch pieces. Cut the kernels off the cobs and chop the grilled onions; add to the steak in the bowl. Add the black beans, kidney beans, jalapeños, chipotle pepper, chicken broth or water, lime zest, and the remaining 4 tablespoons lime juice. Toss to mix well.

★ LAYER THE CASSEROLE: In the bottom of a 9-by-13-inch or 3-quart casserole dish, place 2 tortillas. Sprinkle with 2/3 cup Monterey Jack cheese. Spoon one-third of the steak and bean mixture evenly over the cheese, and top with one-third of the tomato slices and 1/2 teaspoon of the oregano. Repeat, using all the ingredients and making 2 more layers, ending with tomato slices and oregano.

★ BAKE AND SERVE: Cover the casserole with aluminum foil and bake for 20 minutes. Uncover and bake until the filling is bubbly and the cheese has melted—about 10 minutes more. Serve immediately.

NUTRITION INFORMATION PER SERVING—protein: 33.5 g; fat: 19.4 g; carbohydrate: 35.6 g; fiber: 7.4 g; sodium: 667 mg; cholesterol: 75.8 mg; calories: 441.

Take the chill out of any winter night by serving up a generous pot of this classic stew. Spoon it over a bed of egg noodles or accompany with a loaf of crusty French bread.

Beef and Red-Wine Stew

5 slices applewood smoked bacon

4 pounds lean boneless beef chuck, well-trimmed and cut into 2-inch cubes

1/3 cup all-purpose flour

1–2 tablespoons olive oil

2 medium onions, chopped (about 2 cups)

1 tablespoon chopped garlic

3 cups dry red wine (such as cabernet sauvignon or pinot noir)

1 28-ounce can diced tomatoes

1 cup low-sodium beef broth

2 tablespoons red wine vinegar

1 bay leaf

1 teaspoon coarse-ground black pepper

3/4 teaspoon salt

★ COOK THE BACON: Preheat oven to 325°F. In a large Dutch oven, cook the bacon over medium-high heat until crisp and browned. Transfer the bacon to paper towels to drain. Pour off half of the bacon drippings and reserve.

★ BROWN THE BEEF: In a large bowl, dredge the beef in the flour; reserve the bowl. Add 1 tablespoon of the olive to the Dutch oven with the drippings and heat over medium-high heat. Add the beef, in batches, browning it on all sides, adding the reserved 1 tablespoon olive and the reserved bacon drippings to the pan if needed. Transfer the browned beef to the reserved bowl.

★ FINISH THE STEW: Add the onions to the Dutch oven and sauté over medium-high heat until golden—about 5 minutes. Add the garlic and cook for 2 more minutes. Crumble the bacon and add with the remaining ingredients and the browned beef and any juices. Bring to a simmer. Cover and transfer to the oven and bake until the beef is very tender—about 2¼ hours. Remove and discard the bay leaf. Serve the stew hot.

NUTRITION INFORMATION PER SERVING — protein: 52.7 g; fat: 15.3 g; carbohydrate: 9.3 g; fiber: 1.2 g; sodium: 393 mg; cholesterol: 155 mg; calories: 434.

This beef-based chili hails from cattle country, namely the Lone Star State, where cowboys feasted on it during their long cattle drives. Masa harina de maíz *(sometimes referred to as just* masa harina*) is finely ground corn that is used to thicken the chili just before serving. Look for it in gourmet food shops and Latin American grocery stores.*

Cowboy Chili

1 tablespoon vegetable oil

1 pound boneless beef chuck or
    rump roast, cut into ½-inch cubes

1 very large onion, chopped (about 2 cups)

6 cloves garlic, minced

2 14½-ounce cans low-sodium beef broth

1 tablespoon chili powder

1 teaspoon ground cumin

1 14½-ounce can low-sodium diced
    tomatoes

2 dried ancho chiles

1 tablespoon *masa harina de maíz*

1 cup water

2 15½-ounce cans pinto beans, rinsed
    and drained

1 tablespoon cider vinegar

½ teaspoon salt

★ **BROWN THE MEAT:** In a large Dutch oven, heat the oil over medium-high heat until hot but not smoking. Add the beef and cook until browned—about 5 minutes. Transfer the beef to a bowl, set aside, and reduce the heat to medium.

★ **MAKE THE CHILI:** Add the onion to the Dutch oven and sauté until translucent—3 to 5 minutes. Add the garlic and cook 1 more minute. Return the beef and any juices to the Dutch oven. Gradually add 1 can of the beef broth and deglaze by scraping up the brown bits from the bottom of the Dutch oven. Add the chili powder, cumin, and tomatoes. Reduce the heat to medium-low, cover, and simmer until the beef is very tender—about 1 hour.

★ **PURÉE THE CHILES:** In a small saucepan, bring the remaining 1 can of beef broth to a boil over high heat. Add the ancho chiles and let stand for 15 minutes, covered and off the heat, to hydrate. Remove and discard the stems. Place the chiles and broth in a blender or food processor fitted with a metal blade and blend until smooth—2 to 3 minutes.

★ **FINISH THE CHILI:** In a small bowl, whisk the *masa* and water together. Stir the *masa* mixture into the chili. Add the ancho mixture, pinto beans, vinegar, and salt. Simmer uncovered for 15 minutes. Serve hot.

NUTRITION INFORMATION PER SERVING — protein: 37.7 g; fat: 11.1 g; carbohydrate: 31.6 g; fiber: 11.4 g; sodium: 489 mg; cholesterol: 76.3 mg; calories: 379.

Cubans love their picadillo, the nation's traditional stew. This chili draws on its flavors, derived from ingredients introduced to the West Indies by Spanish settlers. Ground beef is a rich foil for the forthright tastes of cumin, nutmeg, allspice, coffee, and molasses that figure prominently here.

Cuban-Coffee Chili

1½ pounds lean ground beef

2 medium onions, chopped
(about 1½ cups)

2 cloves garlic, minced

2 bay leaves

2 teaspoons chili powder

1 teaspoon ground cumin

½ teaspoon ground nutmeg

¼ teaspoon ground allspice

¼ teaspoon chopped fresh thyme leaves

1 teaspoon salt

¼ teaspoon ground black pepper

2 cups strong coffee

1 14½-ounce can diced tomatoes

2 4½-ounce cans diced green chiles

2 tablespoons chopped pimiento-stuffed
green olives

1 tablespoon dark molasses

1 teaspoon capers

⅓ cup raisins

½ cup toasted slivered almonds

5 cups hot cooked rice, cornbread,
or tortillas (optional)

★ **BROWN THE MEAT AND VEGETABLES:** In a large Dutch oven, brown the beef over medium-high heat—about 3 minutes. With a slotted spoon, transfer the beef to a bowl and set aside. Reduce the heat to medium-low. Add the onions to the pan drippings and sauté until translucent—about 3 minutes. Add the garlic and cook for 1 minute.

★ **MAKE THE CHILI:** Return the beef and any juices to the Dutch oven. Stir in the bay leaves, chili powder, cumin, nutmeg, allspice, thyme, salt, and pepper. Stir in the coffee, tomatoes, chiles, olives, molasses, and capers. Bring to a boil and reduce the heat to low. Simmer uncovered for 20 minutes.

★ **FINISH THE CHILI:** Add the raisins and simmer uncovered for 10 more minutes. Remove and discard the bay leaves. Garnish with the almonds. Serve hot over cooked rice or with cornbread or tortillas, if desired.

Tip *For the freshest nutmeg flavor, purchase the spice whole and grate it yourself on a nutmeg or microplane grater.*

NUTRITION INFORMATION PER SERVING WITH RICE—protein: 39.7 g; fat: 21 g; carbohydrate: 85.5 g; fiber: 6.2 g; sodium: 864 mg; cholesterol: 49.5 mg; calories: 689.

What better to eat while watching the big game than a bowlful of hearty beef chili? Here, the cumin-and chili-seasoned sirloin is presented in chunks; be sure to cut them into bite-size pieces—the chili should be easy to enjoy with just a spoon.

Texas-Style Chili

2¹/₂ pounds boneless beef top sirloin steak

2 tablespoons vegetable oil

2 medium onions, chopped (about 2 cups)

3 cloves garlic, finely chopped

1 28-ounce can tomato sauce

1 tablespoon chili powder

1 tablespoon ground cumin

2 teaspoons dried oregano

1 teaspoon salt

2 medium green bell peppers, cut into
   1-inch squares

1 10-ounce package frozen
   whole-kernel corn

Corn tortilla chips (optional)

★ **PREPARE THE SIRLOIN:** Trim off any fat from the sirloin and discard. Cut the sirloin into 1-inch cubes.

★ **BROWN THE SIRLOIN:** In a heavy 6-quart stockpot, heat 1 tablespoon of the oil over medium-high heat until hot but not smoking. Add half of the sirloin cubes. Sauté until pieces are browned on all sides—about 5 minutes. Remove the sirloin to a bowl; repeat to brown the remaining sirloin cubes.

★ **COOK THE CHILI:** Add the remaining 1 tablespoon oil to the stockpot; add the onions and sauté until soft and translucent—5 to 7 minutes. Add the garlic and sauté for 1 minute. Return the browned sirloin and any juices to saucepot. Stir in the tomato sauce, chili powder, cumin, oregano, and salt. Bring the chili to a boil over high heat; reduce the heat to low, cover, and simmer for 1 hour, stirring occasionally.

★ **FINISH THE CHILI:** Stir the bell peppers and corn into the chili mixture. Cover and cook 30 to 45 more minutes or until the meat and vegetables are tender, stirring occasionally.

★ **TO SERVE:** Ladle the chili into soup plates. Garnish with tortilla chips, if desired.

NUTRITION INFORMATION PER SERVING – protein: 44 g; fat: 17 g; carbohydrate: 19 g; fiber: 4 g; sodium: 974 mg; cholesterol: 108 mg; calories: 396.

SKILLET CORNBREAD

If you have a seasoned cast-iron skillet, by all means use it to make this quick bread. A trio of ingredients give it deep corn flavor: cornmeal, creamed corn, and corn kernels.

1 tablespoon butter

1 tablespoon vegetable oil

1 cup all-purpose flour

1 cup yellow or white cornmeal

1 teaspoon baking powder

1 teaspoon baking soda

1 teaspoon salt

1/2 teaspoon cream of tartar

1 8-ounce can cream-style corn

1/2 cup milk

1 large egg

1/2 cup drained canned whole-kernel corn

PREPARE THE SKILLET: Preheat oven to 425°F. Place the butter and vegetable oil in a 9-inch cast-iron skillet (alternatively, use any 9-inch round baking dish). Place the skillet in the oven.

MAKE THE BATTER: In a large bowl, combine the flour, cornmeal, baking powder, baking soda, salt, and cream of tartar. In a medium bowl, combine the cream-style corn, milk, and egg. Stir the milk mixture into the flour mixture just until combined. Fold in the corn kernels.

BAKE THE CORNBREAD: Remove the skillet from the oven and carefully spoon the batter into it. Bake the cornbread until the center feels firm when gently pressed—20 to 25 minutes. Serve warm.

NUTRITION INFORMATION PER SERVING – protein: 5 g; fat: 5 g; carbohydrate: 34 g; fiber: 3 g; sodium: 521 mg; cholesterol: 32 mg; calories: 198.

The addition of Polish sausage to this molasses and brown sugar–sweetened New England classic makes it hearty enough to serve by the bowl accompanied by Skillet Cornbread, opposite, or brown bread.

Baked Beans with Kielbasa

1 16-ounce package dried
    Great Northern beans

1 tablespoon olive oil

1 1-pound low-fat kielbasa, cut into
    1/2-inch rounds

1 large onion, chopped

4 cloves garlic, sliced

1 28-ounce can whole tomatoes
    with thick tomato puree

Boiling water

1/4 cup light molasses

1/4 cup packed light brown sugar

1 teaspoon ground ginger

1 teaspoon salt

1/2 teaspoon ground black pepper

★ **SORT AND SOAK THE BEANS:** Sort and rinse the beans following package directions. Place the beans and 4 cups cold water in a 2-quart saucepan. Bring to a boil over high heat. Remove the saucepan from the heat; cover and set aside 1 hour. Drain and rinse the soaked beans.

★ **BAKE AND SERVE:** Preheat oven to 350°F. In a heavy 6-quart Dutch oven, heat the olive oil over medium heat. Add the kielbasa and sauté until the pieces are browned on all sides. Add the onion and garlic; sauté until lightly browned. Add the drained soaked beans, the tomatoes with puree, 2 cups boiling water, the molasses, brown sugar, ginger, salt, and pepper. Bring to a boil over high heat. Cover and transfer to the oven. Bake the beans for 2 to 2 1/2 hours, until tender. Check the beans occasionally as they bake and, if dry, add more boiling water. Serve hot.

NUTRITION INFORMATION PER SERVING — protein: 22 g; fat: 18 g; carbohydrate: 57 g; fiber: 14 g; sodium: 1,486 mg; cholesterol: 38 mg; calories: 470.

A toss of finely chopped garlic, parsley, and lemon zest—the classic northern Italian preparation known as gremolata— *infuses this elegant dish with bright flavor. Perfect cold-weather dinner party fare, it becomes a meal when served with crusty bread and a simple salad.*

Veal Stew

2 tablespoons olive oil

1 10-ounce package yellow pearl onions, peeled

1 10-ounce package button mushrooms, halved

2 portabella mushrooms, halved and sliced

1 1/2 pounds boneless veal loin or shoulder, cut into 1 1/4-inch cubes

4 cloves garlic, sliced, plus 2 large cloves, finely chopped

3 cups water

1/2 teaspoon chopped fresh rosemary leaves

3/4 teaspoon salt

1/8 teaspoon ground black pepper

1 cup dry white wine

2 tablespoons all-purpose flour

1 pound baby potatoes, scrubbed and halved

1 1-pound package peeled baby carrots

1 pound zucchini (2 medium), cut crosswise into 1/2-inch slices

1/3 cup chopped fresh parsley leaves

1 tablespoon grated lemon zest

★ **BROWN THE MUSHROOMS AND ONIONS:** In a heavy 6-quart stockpot, heat 1 tablespoon of the olive oil over medium heat. Add the pearl onions and mushrooms; sauté until lightly browned—about 5 minutes. Remove the sautéed onions and mushrooms to a small bowl and set aside.

★ **COOK THE STEW:** Add the remaining 1 tablespoon olive oil and the veal to stockpot; sauté until the pieces are browned on all sides—about 5 minutes. Stir in the sliced garlic and sauté until it begins to brown. Add the water, rosemary, salt, and pepper. Bring the stew to a boil over high heat; reduce the heat to low, cover, and simmer for 45 minutes.

★ **ADD THE VEGETABLES:** In a 1-cup measuring cup or small bowl, combine the wine and flour. Stir the mixture into the stew. Add the potatoes, carrots, and the sautéed onions and mushrooms. Cover and bring to a boil over high heat; reduce the heat to low and cook for 20 minutes, stirring occasionally. Add the zucchini and cook until the veal is very tender, 15 more minutes, stirring occasionally.

★ **PREPARE THE *GREMOLATA*:** In a small bowl, combine the finely chopped garlic, parsley, and lemon zest. (Use immediately or cover tightly and refrigerate until ready to serve.)

★ **TO SERVE:** Ladle the stew into soup plates. Top each with a little *gremolata* and serve with the remaining *gremolata*.

NUTRITION INFORMATION PER SERVING — protein: 34 g; fat: 21 g; carbohydrate: 39 g; fiber: 7 g; sodium: 384 mg; cholesterol: 111 mg; calories: 507.

There's nothing like lamb roasting in the oven, fragrant with rosemary and root vegetables, to entice family and friends to the table. Here, the meat is rubbed with a generous amount of garlic that's been pounded into a paste, then nestled in a medley of colorful root vegetables and roasted.

Butterflied Leg of Lamb with Fall Root Vegetables

1 6-pound leg of lamb, butterflied and
   well trimmed

4 cloves garlic, peeled

1³/₄ teaspoons salt

¹/₂ cup packed fresh mint leaves, chopped

2 tablespoons fresh chopped
   rosemary leaves

1¹/₂ tablespoons cracked black
   peppercorns

¹/₄ cup plus 3 tablespoons olive oil

24 baby red potatoes, scrubbed

4 parsnips, peeled and cut into
   2-inch pieces

4 medium carrots, peeled and cut into
   2-inch rounds

16 baby turnips, peeled

¹/₂ teaspoon ground black pepper

¹/₄ cup (¹/₂ stick) butter

1 tablespoon chopped fresh parsley leaves

★ **PREPARE THE LAMB:** Place the lamb cut side up on a work surface. In a small bowl, sprinkle the garlic with ¹/₂ teaspoon of the salt, and use a fork to mash the garlic to a paste. Spread the garlic paste evenly over the lamb and sprinkle with the mint and 1 tablespoon chopped rosemary. Roll the meat from the long side and tie at 2-inch intervals with kitchen twine, and then tie lengthwise. Rub the remaining 1 tablespoon rosemary and the cracked peppercorns into the meat. Place in a shallow roasting pan and drizzle with ¹/₄ cup olive oil. Cover with plastic wrap. Refrigerate for 10 to 24 hours.

★ **ROAST THE LAMB:** Heat the oven to 450°F. Bring the lamb to room temperature in the roasting pan. Sprinkle with ³/₄ teaspoon salt, place on the lowest rack of the oven, and roast for 15 minutes. Reduce oven temperature to 325°F and roast for 45 more minutes. In a large bowl, mix the potatoes, parsnips, carrots, and turnips with the remaining 3 tablespoons olive oil, remaining ¹/₂ teaspoon salt, and the ground black pepper. Scatter the vegetables around the lamb and roast until a meat thermometer inserted into the thickest part of the lamb reaches 140°F—30 to 40 more minutes. Let the lamb rest for 15 minutes before slicing. Toss the vegetables with the butter and parsley and serve the sliced meat with the pan juices.

NUTRITION INFORMATION PER SERVING — protein: 79 g; fat: 33.2 g; carbohydrate: 81.5 g; fiber: 16.3 g; sodium: 812 mg; cholesterol: 233 mg; calories: 941.

The lamb, slow cooked in moist heat, literally falls away from the shank in this robust Mediterranean-inspired dish. The gremolata garnish adds piquant flavor and bright color. Serve the lamb shanks in rimmed soup bowls and pass a peasant loaf for sopping up every bit of the bean "stew."

Savory Braised Lamb Shanks

2 cups dried Great Northern beans (see Note)

1/4 cup all-purpose flour

1 teaspoon paprika

1/2 teaspoon salt

1/4 teaspoon ground black pepper

4 lamb shanks, about 1 1/4 pounds each

4 tablespoons vegetable oil

2 medium onions, chopped (about 2 cups)

5 cloves garlic, chopped

3 cups beef broth

3 cups low-sodium chicken broth

1 1/2 cups dry red wine

1 tablespoon tomato paste

2 bay leaves

1 tablespoon chopped fresh rosemary leaves

1 teaspoon chopped fresh sage leaves

2 large carrots, cut into 1/2-inch chunks (about 1 cup)

2 tablespoons chopped fresh parsley leaves

2 tablespoons grated lemon zest

★ **SOAK THE BEANS:** Sort and rinse the beans following the package directions. In a 4-quart saucepan, bring the beans and cold water to cover to a boil over high heat. Remove the saucepan from the heat; cover and set aside for 1 hour. Drain and rinse the soaked beans.

★ **DREDGE THE SHANKS:** In a shallow bowl, combine the flour, paprika, salt, and pepper. Dredge the lamb shanks in the flour mixture, shaking off the excess.

★ **BROWN THE SHANKS:** In an 8-quart Dutch oven, heat 2 tablespoons of the oil over medium heat. Add the lamb and brown thoroughly on all sides. Remove from the pan and set aside.

★ **BRAISE THE SHANKS:** Pour off the drippings from the pan. Add the remaining 2 tablespoons oil and heat. Add the onions and sauté until softened and lightly browned—5 to 7 minutes. Add 3 cloves of the garlic, the beef broth, chicken broth, 1 cup of the red wine, the tomato paste, bay leaves, rosemary, and sage. Bring to a boil over high heat. Reduce the heat to low and simmer for 5 minutes. Add the reserved beans and the lamb and any juices. Cover and cook for 1 1/2 hours.

★ **FINISH THE STEW:** Stir in the remaining 1/2 cup wine and the carrots. Cover and cook until the carrots are tender—about 30 minutes. In a small bowl, combine the remaining 2 cloves chopped garlic, the parsley, and lemon zest.

★ **TO SERVE:** Remove and discard the bay leaves. Divide the beans among 4 serving plates. Top each with a lamb shank and garnish with the parsley-lemon zest mixture.

NUTRITION INFORMATION PER SERVING – protein: 109 g; fat: 40 g; carbohydrate: 87 g; fiber: 6 g; sodium: 1,665 mg; cholesterol: 255 mg; calories: 1,214.

NOTE: *If you prefer, use four 15-ounce cans Great Northern beans, rinsed and drained, instead of the dried beans. Omit the first step and add the beans in "Finish the Stew," along with the remaining wine and the carrots. Continue with the recipe as directed.*

Garam masala, a blend of ground spices from northern India, gives intensity and heat to this beautiful fusion-cuisine chili. There are dozens of variations on the spice mix, but most typically contain coriander, cumin, cinnamon, black pepper, and cloves. It is sold at many supermarkets and Indian groceries.

Indian-Spiced Lamb Chili

1 tablespoon garam masala

2 teaspoons chili powder

1 teaspoon ground cumin

1 tablespoon vegetable oil

2 pounds boneless lamb leg or shoulder, cut into 1/2-inch pieces

1 large red onion, chopped (about 1 1/4 cups)

2 14 1/2-ounce cans low-sodium beef broth

3 cups water

2 15 1/2-ounce cans black beans, rinsed and drained

1 14 1/2-ounce can low-sodium diced tomatoes

1/2 teaspoon salt

4 cups hot cooked yellow or white rice or naan or pita bread (optional)

★ **ROAST THE SPICES AND BROWN THE MEAT:** In a large Dutch oven, over medium-high heat, toast the garam masala, chili powder, and cumin, stirring constantly, until fragrant. Add the oil and stir well. Stir in the lamb and cook until browned on all sides—about 4 minutes. Remove the lamb to a bowl and set aside.

★ **SIMMER THE CHILI:** In the same Dutch oven, sauté the onion until translucent—2 to 3 minutes. Add the lamb and any juices, the beef broth, and water. Reduce the heat to medium-low, cover, and simmer until the lamb is tender—about 45 minutes.

★ **FINISH THE CHILI:** Add the black beans, tomatoes, and salt. Reduce the heat to low, cover, and simmer for 30 more minutes. Serve hot over cooked rice or with naan or pita bread, if desired.

Tip *If bone-in lamb leg or shoulder is all that is available, ask the butcher to cut it into 1/2-inch pieces for you save yourself prep time.*

NUTRITION INFORMATION PER SERVING WITH RICE—protein: 99.7 g; fat: 30.9 g; carbohydrate: 97.1 g; fiber: 16.2 g; sodium: 975 mg; cholesterol: 245 mg; calories: 908.

Tip Serve this dish with Skillet Cornbread (see page 26). Pour the bacon drippings into a tempered glass jar and reserve for using in place of the butter and oil in the corn bread.

This dish starts with the classic combination of pork chops and applesauce and then takes it to another level by adding hard cider to the mix and a garnish of crumbled bacon. Use a crisp, sweet apple such as Gala, Criterion, or Mutsu to complement the smoky pork and autumn vegetables.

Smoky Pork Chops with Cabbage and Apples

5 slices bacon

2 tablespoons olive oil

4 bone-in pork loin chops (about 1³/₄ pounds)

1¹/₄ teaspoons salt

³/₄ teaspoon ground black pepper

Flour for dredging

1 large onion, finely chopped

3 cloves garlic, finely chopped

1 medium head green cabbage (about 1¹/₂ pounds), cut in half, cored, and sliced crosswise into shreds (about 10 cups)

2 large carrots, cut into thin slices on the diagonal

2 large apples (about 1 pound), peeled, cored, and thinly sliced

3 small bay leaves

¹/₂ cup hard cider or dry French vermouth

★ **COOK THE BACON:** In a large skillet, cook the bacon over medium heat until browned and crisp. Drain the bacon on paper towels. Pour out all but 2 tablespoons of bacon drippings and add the olive oil to the skillet. Set the pan aside.

★ **COOK THE CHOPS:** Season the pork chops with ¹/₄ teaspoon salt and ¹/₄ teaspoon pepper and dredge the pork chops in the flour. Heat the skillet of drippings over medium heat. Add the pork chops and cook on both sides until browned—about 8 minutes. Remove the chops from the skillet and set aside.

★ **COOK THE CABBAGE MIXTURE:** Add the onion and garlic to the skillet. Cook, stirring, until the onion softens—about 3 minutes. Add the cabbage, carrots, apples, bay leaves, hard cider, remaining 1 teaspoon salt, and remaining ¹/₂ teaspoon pepper. Stir well to combine, cover, and bring the mixture to a boil. Uncover the pan and place the chops on top of the cabbage mixture. Re-cover and return to a boil. Reduce the heat to medium and cook until the chops are tender—20 to 25 minutes.

★ **TO SERVE:** Chop the reserved bacon coarsely and sprinkle over the pork and cabbage. Remove the bay leaves before serving.

NUTRITION INFORMATION PER SERVING — protein: 71 g; fat: 41 g; carbohydrate: 35 g; fiber: 9 g; sodium: 989 mg; cholesterol: 216 mg; calories: 819.

Chose a spicy sausage, such as merguez or chorizo, for this soul-satisfying hash seasoned with warm spices, including cinnamon and cumin. Serve with a poached egg on top for brunch or with a salad of chopped parsley, mint, cucumber, and tomato for dinner.

Potato and Sausage Hash with Moroccan Flavors

3 tablespoons olive oil

9 ounces sausage, such as merguez or chorizo, cut into 1/4-inch-thick rounds

2 medium onions, sliced 1/4-inch thick

1 3/4 pounds baby Yukon Gold potatoes, scrubbed and halved

1/2 teaspoon ground cumin

1/4 teaspoon ground cinnamon

1/4 teaspoon crushed red pepper

1 preserved lemon, cut into 12 wedges (about 3 ounces)

★ COOK THE SAUSAGE AND ONIONS: In a large skillet, heat 1 tablespoon of the olive oil over medium heat. Add the sausage slices and cook until browned—about 4 minutes. Remove from the pan and set aside. Heat the remaining 2 tablespoons olive oil in the skillet over medium heat, add the onions, and cook until softened—about 5 minutes.

★ FINISH THE HASH: Add the potatoes and cook, turning occasionally until they begin to brown—about 10 more minutes. Add the cumin, cinnamon, crushed red pepper, preserved lemon, and the browned sausage, and cook until the potatoes are deep golden—about 3 more minutes. Reduce the heat to medium-low, cover, and cook until the potatoes are tender and easily pierced with a fork—25 to 30 minutes. Serve hot or warm.

Tip *Preserved lemons are lemons that have been pickled in salt and their own juices. They can be found in Middle Eastern and specialty gourmet markets.*

NUTRITION INFORMATION PER SERVING—protein: 10 g; fat: 18 g; carbohydrate: 21 g; fiber: 1.7 g; sodium: 543 mg; cholesterol: 28 mg; calories: 294.

There's no better way to mark the weekend than with a skillet of hash cooking in the kitchen. This uses leftover cooked potatoes—perhaps the best way to make any hash—and thick cubes of slab bacon.

Bacon and Egg Hash

1/2 **pound slab bacon, cut into**
   1/2-**inch cubes**

1 **large onion, coarsely chopped**

1 **red bell pepper, coarsely chopped**

11/2 **pounds leftover cooked potatoes,**
   chopped

4 **large eggs**

★ MAKE THE HASH: In a large heavy skillet, cook the bacon over medium-high heat until browned and crisp. With a slotted spoon, remove the bacon to paper towels and set aside. Discard all but 2 tablespoons of the bacon drippings. Add the onion and bell pepper to the skillet and sauté for 3 minutes. Add the potatoes and browned bacon and cook until the potatoes are heated through—about 5 minutes. Reduce the heat to medium-low and gently crack the eggs onto the surface of the hash. Cover the pan and cook until the eggs are set—about 5 minutes. Serve immediately.

> **Tip** *Don't be tempted to use thin-sliced bacon for this recipe; it doesn't have the same texture as its thick-cut counterpart, which is essential to stand up to the potatoes.*

NUTRITION INFORMATION PER SERVING— protein: 20.5 g; fat: 19.2 g; carbohydrate: 25.3 g; fiber: 3.8 g; sodium: 929 mg; cholesterol: 243 mg; calories: 359.

A pressure cooker frees you from having to constantly stir the risotto. With as little as 2 minutes spent stirring at the end of the cooking time, this richly flavored rice dish is speedy enough to make on a busy weeknight.

Porcini-Pancetta Risotto

1½ **ounces dried porcini mushrooms**

6 **ounces pancetta, chopped**

1 **medium onion, chopped (about 1 cup)**

2 **tablespoons finely chopped garlic**

1½ **cups arborio rice**

½ **cup Marsala wine**

2½ **cups low-sodium chicken broth**

½ **teaspoon finely chopped fresh rosemary leaves**

1 **teaspoon salt**

½ **teaspoon ground black pepper**

½ **cup grated Asiago cheese**

2 **teaspoons finely grated lemon zest**

1 **teaspoon finely chopped fresh parsley leaves**

★ REHYDRATE THE MUSHROOMS: Place the mushrooms in a medium bowl, add 1½ cups of boiling water, and steep until soft—about 15 minutes. Use a slotted spoon to remove the mushrooms, reserving the broth. Roughly chop the mushrooms and set aside. Pour the mushroom liquid through a very fine strainer or cheesecloth and reserve.

★ MAKE THE RISOTTO: In a pressure cooker, cook the pancetta over medium-high heat until lightly browned. Add the onion and garlic and cook until soft. Stir in the rice, add the Marsala, and continue to cook until most of the liquid has been absorbed—about 2 minutes. Add the mushrooms, reserved mushroom broth, chicken broth, rosemary, salt, and pepper. Seal the pressure-cooker lid and bring the cooker to high pressure. Reduce the heat just enough to maintain high pressure and cook for 7 minutes. Turn off the heat, quick-release the pressure, and carefully remove the lid. Over medium-high heat, stir the rice constantly until it becomes creamy and thick—1 to 2 minutes. Remove from the heat and stir in the Asiago cheese and lemon zest. Garnish with the parsley and serve immediately.

Tip If the words "pressure cooker" conjure up images of food splattered on the kitchen ceiling, you haven't caught up with the latest designs. Now equipped with safety features that make it impossible to open them if there is even a trace of pressure inside, modern pressure cookers are a boon for the time-pressed cook.

NUTRITION INFORMATION PER SERVING—protein: 14.8 g; fat: 8.9 g; carbohydrate: 45.8 g; fiber: 2.7 g; sodium: 821 mg; cholesterol: 24.8 mg; calories: 336.

Inspired by the Louisiana Cajun version of smoked meat, vegetables, and rice, this classic one-pot preparation calls for smoked pork shoulder. If time is a factor, ask your butcher to cut the shoulder into ½-inch cubes for you. Before you begin, be sure that the 3-quart heatproof glass bowl or casserole fits inside the stockpot or steamer you are using.

Jerked Jambalaya

¾ teaspoon ground allspice

¾ teaspoon chili powder

½ teaspoon salt

¼ teaspoon ground cinnamon

¼ teaspoon garlic powder

¼ teaspoon ground nutmeg

¼ teaspoon ground black pepper

½ pound smoked pork shoulder, cut into
  ½-inch cubes

1 cup long-grain white rice

2 large carrots, peeled and cut into
  ½-inch chunks

1 stalk celery, cut into ¼-inch slices

1 small red bell pepper, cut into
  ¼-inch strips

1 tablespoon olive oil

1 cup boiling water

1½ cups chopped broccoli

1 cup cooked black-eyed peas

★ **PREPARE THE JERK SEASONING:** In a small cup, combine the allspice, chili powder, salt, cinnamon, garlic powder, nutmeg, and black pepper.

★ **MIX THE INGREDIENTS:** In a 3-quart ovenproof glass dish or casserole, combine the pork, rice, carrots, celery, bell pepper, olive oil, and jerk seasoning; stir to mix well.

★ **STEAM THE JAMBALAYA:** In an 8-quart stockpot, place a wire rack or steaming basket and add 1½ inches water. Place the glass dish with the jambalaya on the rack. Stir the boiling water into the jambalaya. Cover and bring the water in the saucepot to a boil over high heat. Reduce the heat to medium-low and steam for 20 minutes.

★ **CONTINUE COOKING:** Uncover the stockpot; with a large spoon, stir the jambalaya, making sure to mix the liquid at the bottom of the dish into the rice and vegetables. Cover and steam for 15 minutes. Uncover; stir in the broccoli and black-eyed peas. Cover and steam 10 more minutes, or until the rice and vegetables are cooked through. If using an automatic steamer, follow manufacturer's directions.

★ **TO SERVE:** Remove the jambalaya from the stockpot to a wire rack. Cover with a lid or aluminum foil and let stand for 10 minutes before serving.

NUTRITION INFORMATION PER SERVING — protein: 17 g; fat: 8 g; carbohydrate: 35 g; fiber: 5 g; sodium: 361 mg; cholesterol: 43 mg; calories: 278.

There's nothing better to chase a winter chill than a piping hot bowl of this soup, based on the Portuguese staple. While the original version features Galician cabbage, a large, deep-green variety with crinkled leaves, also known as dinosaur or black kale, any thinly sliced kale will taste delicious.

Kale Potato Soup

1 pound fully cooked smoked sausage

1 tablespoon olive oil

1 large onion, chopped

2 cloves garlic, chopped

2 14½-ounce cans low-sodium
   chicken broth

2 cups water

2 bay leaves

2 pounds baking potatoes, peeled
   and diced

1 pound 'Lacinato' or any other
   kale variety

¼ teaspoon ground black pepper

★ START THE SOUP: Cut the sausage into ¼-inch-thick rounds. In a 5-quart stockpot, heat the olive oil over medium heat. Add the sausage and sauté until lightly browned. Remove the sausage to a plate; set aside. Add the onion and garlic to the saucepot; sauté for 1 minute. Stir in the chicken broth, water, bay leaves, and potatoes. Cover and bring to a boil over high heat. Reduce the heat to low and simmer the soup for 45 minutes or until the potatoes are very tender.

★ PREPARE THE KALE: Meanwhile, cut off and discard the lower stems of the kale leaves. Stack a handful of leaves and press down tightly. With a sharp knife, very thinly slice the leaves crosswise; set the sliced leaves aside. Repeat with the balance of the leaves.

★ FINISH THE SOUP AND SERVE: Remove the stockpot from the heat. Discard the bay leaves. With a potato masher, mash the potatoes in the soup. Return the soup to medium heat and bring to a boil. Stir in the browned sausage slices, the kale, and pepper. Cook, uncovered, until the kale leaves are tender—about 3 minutes. Ladle the soup into serving bowls.

NUTRITION INFORMATION PER SERVING—protein: 14 g; fat: 18 g; carbohydrate: 30 g; fiber: 5 g; sodium: 1,005 mg; cholesterol: 38 mg; calories: 338.

A delightful combination of both sweet and savory ingredients flavors this wintry stew of tender pork, carrots, and parsnips; plump prunes and orange juice sweeten it all.

Pork and Vegetables with Dried Fruit

2¹/₂ **pounds boneless pork shoulder blade or butt roast**

2 **teaspoons vegetable oil**

2 **medium onions, chopped (about 2 cups)**

1 **14¹/₂-ounce can chicken broth**

1 **cup orange juice**

¹/₂ **teaspoon ground allspice**

¹/₂ **teaspoon salt**

¹/₂ **teaspoon ground black pepper**

3 **large carrots, peeled and cut into 1-inch slices**

3 **large parsnips, peeled and cut into 1-inch slices**

1 **cup pitted prunes**

2 **tablespoons cider vinegar**

★ TRIM AND CUBE THE PORK: Trim off any fat from the pork and discard. Cut the pork into 1-inch cubes.

★ SIMMER THE STEW: In a heavy 6-quart stockpot, heat the oil over medium-high heat. Add half of the pork cubes. Sauté until all the pan juices evaporate and the meat is well browned. Remove the pork to a bowl. Repeat to brown the remaining pork cubes. Add the onions and sauté for 3 minutes. Add the chicken broth, orange juice, allspice, salt, and pepper. Return the browned pork and any juices in the bowl to the stockpot. Bring the stew to a boil over high heat; reduce the heat to low, cover, and simmer for 45 minutes, stirring occasionally.

★ FINISH THE STEW: Add the carrots and parsnips. Cook until the pork and vegetables are tender, stirring occasionally—about 30 minutes. Add the prunes and vinegar and cook 15 more minutes. Serve hot.

NUTRITION INFORMATION PER SERVING — protein: 38 g; fat: 18 g; carbohydrate: 22 g; fiber: 4 g; sodium: 712 mg; cholesterol: 131 mg; calories: 405.

Literally translated, pot-au-feu is French for "pot on fire," and is the classic Gallic boiled dinner. Here, two lesser-known root vegetables, kohlrabi and black radishes, are added to the mix of parsnips and savoy cabbage. Kohlrabi's crisp flavor falls somewhere between a turnip and cabbage, while black radishes boast a bold, pronounced bite.

Pork Shoulder Pot-au-Feu

3 bay leaves, preferably fresh

3 sprigs fresh thyme

2 cloves garlic, peeled and crushed with
    the side of a large knife

1 teaspoon whole allspice berries

1 teaspoon whole black peppercorns

1 whole clove

24 cups (6 quarts) water

2 tablespoons salt

1 6-pound pork shoulder, tied with
    kitchen twine

3 small kohlrabi, peeled and cut in half

2 parsnips, peeled and cut into
    3-inch pieces

3 medium carrots, peeled and cut into
    3-inch pieces

1 large black radish, scrubbed and cut
    into 6 wedges

1 small head savoy cabbage, cut into
    6 wedges with stem end attached

Mustard

Coarse salt

★ **COOK THE PORK:** Place the bay leaves, thyme, garlic, allspice, pepper-corns, and clove in a square of cheesecloth and tie with kitchen twine to form a sachet. In a large stockpot, bring the water and salt to a boil over high heat. Add the spice sachet and pork shoulder, making sure the water covers the meat. Reduce the heat to low and simmer, with the cover slightly ajar, skim-ming the surface occasionally, until the pork is very tender and easily pierced with a fork—about 3³/₄ hours. Transfer the pork to a large plate and keep warm. Reserve the broth.

★ **COOK THE VEGETABLES:** Strain the broth through a cheesecloth-lined strainer and return to the stockpot. Add the kohlrabi, parsnips, carrots, and radish. Bring to a boil over high heat; reduce the heat to medium-low and cook for 15 minutes. Add the cabbage and continue to cook until all vegetables are tender—about 15 more minutes. With tongs or a slotted spoon, lift the vegeta-bles from the liquid and keep warm. Slice the pork or pull into pieces. Arrange the pork and vegetables on a deep serving platter. Serve with the cooking broth, mustard, and coarse salt.

NUTRITION INFORMATION PER SERVING — protein: 84 g; fat: 31.3 g; carbohydrate: 10.7 g; fiber: 3.2 g; sodium: 421 mg; cholesterol: 292 mg; calories: 678.

There's little more involved here than browning sausage, peppers, and onions, then tossing the remaining ingredients in the pot to cook over low heat for less than 30 minutes. Andouille, a Cajun smoked specialty, is especially spicy; substitute smoked kielbasa for a milder chili. Serve in deep soup bowls, spooned over white rice.

Andouille and Black-Eyed Pea Chili

1 tablespoon vegetable oil

1 pound andouille sausage, cut into
    1/4-inch cubes

3 medium yellow onions, chopped
    (about 2 cups)

1 large red bell pepper, chopped
    (about 1 1/2 cups)

1 bay leaf

2 15 1/2-ounce cans black-eyed peas,
    rinsed and drained

2 14 1/2-ounce cans low-sodium beef broth

2 teaspoons chili powder

1 teaspoon ground cumin

1 teaspoon chopped fresh thyme leaves

1 tablespoon chopped fresh parsley leaves

1/2 teaspoon salt

6 cups hot cooked rice or biscuits or
    corn muffins (optional)

★ BROWN THE SAUSAGE AND VEGETABLES: In a large Dutch oven, heat the oil over medium-high heat until hot but not smoking. Add the sausage and cook, stirring occasionally, until browned—5 to 7 minutes. Pour off the excess fat. Add the onions and bell pepper and cook until the onions are golden brown—5 to 6 minutes.

★ MAKE THE CHILI: Add the bay leaf, black-eyed peas, and beef broth, stirring well. Add the chili powder, cumin, and thyme. Bring to a boil and reduce the heat to low. Simmer, uncovered, for 25 minutes.

★ TO SERVE: Add the parsley and salt, stirring well. Discard the bay leaf. Serve hot over cooked rice, or with buscuits or corn muffins, if desired.

Tip If you want to use dried black-eyed peas, first sort through them and discard any small stones. Soak them overnight in cold water to cover, in the refrigerator. Drain and discard the soaking water before cooking the beans. For the quick-soak method, pour the beans into boiling water and boil for 2 minutes. Remove from the stove and allow to stand for 1 hour, then drain.

NUTRITION INFORMATION PER SERVING WITH RICE—protein: 24 g; fat: 25 g; carbohydrate: 96.4 g; fiber: 10 g; sodium: 1,052 mg; cholesterol: 50.6 mg; calories: 715.

Green tomatillos, roasted poblanos, and cilantro replace tomatoes in this bright, mildly spicy stew, made hearty with cubed pork. Once the peppers have been roasted, it can be prepared in just about an hour. Serve with charred tortillas, a traditional southwestern accompaniment.

Chili Verde

2 tablespoons vegetable oil

1¹/₂ cups chopped onions

3 cloves garlic, chopped

1 jalapeño pepper, seeded and chopped

1 teaspoon ground cumin

1 pound tomatillos, husks removed, rinsed, and quartered

6 poblano or Italian frying peppers, roasted, peeled, seeded, and chopped (see below)

3 cups low-sodium chicken broth

1 large potato, peeled and cut into 1-inch cubes

¹/₃ cup chopped fresh cilantro leaves

1 teaspoon salt

¹/₄ teaspoon ground black pepper

2 pounds boneless pork chops, cut into 1-inch cubes

★ **MAKE THE TOMATILLO MIXTURE:** In a 6-quart stockpot, heat the oil over medium heat. Add the onions and sauté until softened—5 to 7 minutes. Add the garlic, jalapeño, and cumin; sauté 2 more minutes. Add the tomatillos, poblano peppers, and chicken broth. Increase the heat to high and bring the mixture to a boil. Cook for 1 minute. Reduce the heat to low and simmer until the tomatillos are soft—about 20 minutes. Transfer the tomatillo mixture to a bowl and let cool for 10 minutes.

★ **PROCESS THE MIXTURE:** In a food processor fitted with a metal blade, in batches, pulse the mixture until coarsely processed. Return the processed mixture to the stockpot.

★ **COOK AND SERVE:** Add the potato, cilantro, salt, and black pepper. Cook over medium heat until the potato is fork-tender—about 15 minutes. Stir in the pork and cook just until the pork has cooked through—10 to 15 minutes. Serve hot.

ROASTING CHILE PEPPERS

Roasted chile peppers give Chili Verde its smoky edge. Mildly spicy when fresh, poblano chiles develop an almost sweet flavor when roasted; Italian frying peppers make a good substitute. When working with any chile pepper, it's a good idea to wear rubber gloves.

To roast a pepper, place it directly over a medium gas flame, rotating it every few minutes until charred on all sides. Alternatively, roast peppers in your oven on a baking sheet at 400°F, turning them occasionally until charred. Allow the peppers to cool, then peel off the skins.

NUTRITION INFORMATION PER SERVING— protein: 52 g; fat: 26 g; carbohydrate: 24 g; fiber: 4 g; sodium: 862 mg; cholesterol: 148 mg; calories: 544.

Brown sugar sweetens the spicy combination of ginger and chili powder—a mix of ground red chiles, garlic, coriander, cumin, oregano, and cloves—for a deeply fragrant and satisfying dish. Serve this chili with an aromatic rice such as basmati or jasmine.

Sweet and Spicy Pork Chili

1 teaspoon vegetable oil

2 pounds boneless pork chops or pork
    tenderloin, cut into 1/2-inch cubes

2 shallots, coarsely chopped
    (about 1/3 cup)

2 cloves garlic, minced

2 tablespoons chili powder

2 teaspoons crushed red pepper

1 14 1/2-ounce can low-sodium beef broth

1 14-ounce can low-fat coconut milk
    (not cream of coconut)

1 teaspoon peeled grated fresh ginger

3 medium carrots, peeled and sliced on
    the diagonal (about 1 cup)

3 tablespoons frozen orange
    juice concentrate

1 tablespoon low-sodium soy sauce

1/4 cup packed light brown sugar

6 cups hot cooked rice or rice noodles
    or Chinese egg noodles (optional)

Chopped green onions (optional)

★ **BROWN THE MEAT:** In a large Dutch oven, heat the oil over medium-high heat until hot but not smoking. Add the pork and cook until lightly browned—6 to 8 minutes. Remove the pork to a bowl, set aside, and reduce the heat to medium.

★ **MAKE THE CHILI:** Add the shallots to the Dutch oven and sauté until translucent—about 2 minutes. Add the garlic and cook for 1 minute. Add the chili powder, crushed red pepper, beef broth, coconut milk, and ginger. Reduce the heat to low and simmer, uncovered, for 15 minutes. Add the carrots and simmer for 10 more minutes.

★ **FINISH THE CHILI:** Add the orange juice concentrate, soy sauce, and brown sugar. Simmer for 10 minutes. Serve hot over cooked rice or with rice noodles or Chinese noodles and sprinkle with chopped green onions, if desired.

NUTRITION INFORMATION PER SERVING WITH RICE — protein: 55.4 g; fat: 27 g; carbohydrate: 76.4 g; fiber: 3 g; sodium: 209 mg; cholesterol: 118 mg; calories: 779.

The beauty of this savory tart of thinly sliced potatoes and onions, peas, bacon and mild, buttery Jarlsberg is that, depending on the size of the slices, it works equally well as an appetizer or for brunch, lunch, or dinner. Slice it into bite-sized pieces for nibbling with cocktails or serve it with a mixed green salad for a meal.

Onion and Potato Tart

1/2 **17 1/4-ounce package frozen puff pastry, thawed (1 sheet)**

1 large (3/4 pound) baking potato, peeled and sliced crosswise

1 tablespoon olive oil

1/8 teaspoon salt

6 slices (5 ounces) bacon, cut into 1-inch pieces

1 1/2 pounds onions, sliced

1 cup frozen green peas

1 cup shredded Jarlsberg cheese

★ **FORM THE TART SHELL:** Heat oven to 400°F. Unfold the pastry sheet. Between 2 sheets of lightly floured waxed paper, roll out the pastry to a 15-by-12-inch rectangle. Remove the top sheet of waxed paper and turn the pastry into an 11-by-8-inch tart pan with a removable bottom, allowing the excess to extend over the edge. Remove the remaining sheet of waxed paper. Fold the excess pastry inside so that it is even around the top edge with the rim of the pan; press the pastry against the side to make an even thickness. With a sharp knife, trim the pastry even with the edge of the pan, except at the corners. Pinch the pastry at the corners to extend 1/4 inch above the pan.

★ **MAKE THE FILLING:** In a medium bowl, toss the potato with the olive oil and salt. Arrange the potato slices evenly over the bottom of the pastry crust. Bake for 20 minutes.

★ **COOK THE BACON:** Meanwhile, in a large skillet, cook the bacon over medium heat until crisp and brown—about 4 minutes. With a slotted spoon, transfer the bacon to a paper towel to drain. In bacon drippings in skillet, sauté the onions until golden brown and almost tender—about 10 minutes. Fold in the peas and bacon; remove from the heat.

★ **FINISH BAKING THE TART:** Remove the pastry from the oven and top with half the Jarlsberg cheese, the onion mixture, and the remaining cheese. Bake the tart 15 to 20 more minutes or until the pastry is cooked through. If necessary, cover the edges of the pastry with strips of aluminum foil to prevent overbrowning.

★ **TO SERVE:** Remove the rim of the pan from the tart. Cut the tart into 6 pieces.

NUTRITION INFORMATION PER SERVING—protein: 14 g; fat: 20 g; carbohydrate: 264 g; fiber: 7 g; sodium: 362 mg; cholesterol: 23 mg; calories: 424.

In the morning, brown the sausage and bacon and combine it with the remaining ingredients in a slow cooker. Turn on the cooker and forget it for the rest of the day. By dinnertime, you'll have a fragrant, hearty stew ready to serve with warm crusty rolls and a green salad.

Butter Bean and Sausage Hot Pot

(Pictured on page 12)

1 pound smoked sausage
   (such as kielbasa)

1/4 pound sliced bacon

1 large fennel bulb, cut into 2-inch-long
   and 1/4-inch-wide matchsticks (3 cups)

1 cup thickly sliced celery

1 medium onion, coarsely chopped
   (about 1 cup)

2 tablespoons coarsely chopped garlic
   (about 3 cloves)

1 pound dried butter beans,
   sorted and rinsed

1 bay leaf

1 1/2 teaspoons chopped fresh
   rosemary leaves

1/4 teaspoon ground black pepper

5 cups water

2 14 1/2-ounce cans low-sodium
   chicken broth

★ **MAKE THE HOT POT:** In a large skillet, brown the sausage over medium-high heat. Remove the sausage and slice it into 1/2-inch rounds. Set aside. Cook the bacon in the same skillet until crisp and golden brown; remove the bacon from the skillet and set aside, reserving the bacon drippings. Reduce the heat to medium, add the fennel and celery to the bacon drippings, and cook for 4 to 5 minutes. Add the onion and garlic and continue to cook until the onion becomes translucent. Remove from the heat. Place the browned sausage, cooked bacon, sautéed vegetables, and the remaining ingredients in a slow cooker. Cover and cook on the low setting until the butter beans are tender—6 to 8 hours. Remove and discard the bay leaf. Serve hot.

NUTRITION INFORMATION PER SERVING — protein: 17 g; fat: 19 g; carbohydrate: 12.6 g; fiber: 4 g; sodium: 901 mg; cholesterol: 42.7 mg; calories: 290.

Poultry

The ultimate one-dish dinner that no one ever tires of: Master this and you'll never be without a presentable meal to serve friends and family.

Roast Lemon Chicken

3 lemons

1/4 cup (1/2 stick) unsalted butter

1 4-pound whole chicken, rinsed and patted dry

1 teaspoon salt

1/2 teaspoon whole black peppercorns, crushed

6 large garlic cloves, crushed

1/2 pound baby Yukon Gold potatoes, scrubbed and halved

1/2 pound baby carrots

1 medium onion, cut into wedges

★ **PREPARE THE CHICKEN:** Preheat oven to 500°F. Zest and juice 1 of the lemons. Heat the lemon juice and butter in a small saucepan and set aside. Sprinkle the chicken cavity with 1/2 teaspoon of the salt and 1/4 teaspoon of the crushed peppercorns. Gently slide two fingers under the skin of the breast and rub half of the zest and 1/8 teaspoon crushed peppercorns onto the breast meat. Cut 1 lemon into quarters and place it and the garlic cloves in the cavity. Tie the legs together with butcher's twine and season the outside of the bird with the remaining 1/2 teaspoon salt and 1/8 teaspoon crushed peppercorns.

★ **ROAST THE CHICKEN:** Place the chicken in a roasting pan and roast for 10 minutes. Reduce the oven temperature to 375°F. Roast for 30 minutes. Quarter the remaining lemon and scatter the potatoes, baby carrots, onion, and lemon quarters around the chicken in the bottom of the pan. Continue to roast, basting the chicken with the melted butter and lemon mixture every 15 minutes, until a thermometer inserted into the thigh meat reads 165°-170°F—about 45 minutes more.

★ **SERVE THE CHICKEN:** Transfer the chicken and vegetables to a platter. Cover loosely with aluminum foil and let rest for at least 15 minutes to allow the juices to settle. Carve the chicken and serve it accompanied by the vegetables and pan juices.

NUTRITION INFORMATION PER SERVING — protein: 57 g; fat: 63 g; carbohydrate: 5.6 g; fiber: 1.3 g; sodium: 815 mg; cholesterol: 286.5 g mg; calories: 825.

Preserved lemons are available in specialty shops and through various Internet retailers. They're delicious in this dish as well as in other vegetable or fish recipes. Refrigerate unused preserved lemons for up to 2 months.

Preserved-Lemon Chicken

2 preserved lemons

2 fresh lemons

2 tablespoons olive oil

2 tablespoons fresh lemon juice

2 cloves garlic, minced

1/2 teaspoon minced fresh oregano leaves

1/2 teaspoon minced fresh thyme leaves

1/2 teaspoon salt

1/4 teaspoon ground black pepper

1 3 1/2-pound quartered chicken, rinsed, patted dry, and excess fat removed

15 cherry tomatoes

20 small green olives, such as picholine

★ **CUT THE LEMONS:** Preheat oven to 450°F. Cut the 2 preserved lemons into 12 wedges, then cut the wedges crosswise into 1/16-inch-thick slices and set aside. Cut the 2 fresh lemons into 1/2-inch rounds. Coat a large ovenproof skillet with the olive oil and arrange the fresh lemon slices on the bottom of the skillet. Set aside.

★ **MAKE THE CHICKEN:** In a large bowl, mix together lemon juice, garlic, herbs, salt, and pepper; add the chicken pieces and toss to coat well. Place the chicken pieces on top of the lemon slices and roast for 30 minutes. Add the cherry tomatoes, green olives, and preserved lemon slices. Roast for 25 more minutes. Serve hot.

MAKING PRESERVED LEMONS

To make your own preserved lemons, preheat oven to 300°F. Cut 9 lemons into 6 wedges each. In a medium-size ovenproof nonreactive baking dish, toss together lemon wedges, 1/2 cup plus 2 tablespoons sea salt, 1 tablespoon sugar, and 2/3 cup fresh lemon juice. Cover the dish with foil and bake for 2 1/2 hours. Remove from oven and cool completely. Store the preserved lemon wedges for up to 2 months in the refrigerator.

NUTRITION INFORMATION PER SERVING – protein: 86.4 g; fat: 22 g; carbohydrate: 8.9 g; fiber: 2.2 g; sodium: 1,047 mg; cholesterol: 277 mg; calories: 588

When fresh peas are at their sweetest, they dazzle in this one-dish meal. Kernels of corn trimmed straight from the cob make a nice addition, too. First the chicken pieces are seared on the stovetop and then roasted in the oven with new potatoes and fresh peas for a bright, delicately flavored dinner.

Chicken with Fresh Peas and Sparkling Wine

1 3½-pound whole chicken, cut into 8 pieces

1¼ teaspoons fine-grained sea salt

½ teaspoon ground black pepper

2 tablespoons canola oil

1 pound new potatoes, scrubbed and quartered

1 cup chopped onion or leeks

3 cups sparkling white wine

2 cups shelled fresh peas

1 tablespoon unsalted butter

2 tablespoons roughly chopped dill

★ **BROWN THE CHICKEN:** Preheat oven to 350°F. Line a platter with several layers of paper towels and set aside. Season the chicken pieces with the salt and pepper. Heat the oil in a large, ovenproof skillet over medium-high heat until hot but not smoking. Place the chicken pieces skin-side down in the skillet and cook until they are well browned and the skin is crispy—about 5 minutes per side. Remove the chicken to the prepared plate. Discard all but 3 tablespoons of the pan drippings.

★ **FINISH THE DISH:** Place the potatoes in the drippings in the skillet and cook over medium-high heat on one side until browned—about 10 minutes. Add the onion and cook for 2 minutes. Add the sparkling wine and let boil for 1 minute. Return the chicken pieces to the skillet; transfer to the oven and roast uncovered for 40 minutes. Add the peas to the skillet and cook for an additional 5 minutes. Dot the chicken pieces with the butter and let it melt. Sprinkle with the dill and serve immediately.

NUTRITION INFORMATION PER SERVING — protein: 40.8 g; fat: 23.7 g; carbohydrate: 33.7 g; fiber: 4.5 g; sodium: 481 mg; cholesterol: 138 mg; calories: 572.

The quintessential one-pot meal, this savory pie features a classic mix of carrots, celery, pearl onions, and peas. You can substitute any root vegetable for the carrots—just be sure to cut it the same size as the other vegetables so all cook uniformly. Make fast work of dinner by using a packaged piecrust.

Chicken Potpie

1 tablespoon vegetable oil

3/4 pound boneless, skinless chicken thighs, cut into 1 1/2-inch pieces

3/4 pound boneless, skinless chicken breasts, cut into 1 1/2-inch pieces

1 cup frozen pearl onions, thawed

1 cup thinly sliced carrots

1/3 cup thinly sliced celery

1 1/2 cups frozen peas

1 14 1/2-ounce can low-sodium chicken broth

3/4 cup milk

1/3 cup all-purpose flour

1/2 teaspoon poultry seasoning

3/4 teaspoon salt

1/4 teaspoon ground black pepper

Flaky Piecrust (recipe follows) or 1/2 15-ounce package refrigerated piecrust

★ MAKE THE CHICKEN: In a 10-inch cast-iron skillet, heat the oil over medium heat. Add the chicken thighs and cook for 2 minutes. Add the chicken breasts and pearl onions; sauté until the chicken has cooked through and the onions are lightly browned—5 to 7 minutes. Using a slotted spoon, transfer the chicken and onions to a plate and set aside. Preheat oven to 425°F.

★ MAKE THE SAUCE: Add the carrots and celery to the skillet; sauté the vegetables until slightly softened—about 5 minutes. Stir in the peas and chicken broth. Bring to a boil; reduce the heat to low, and simmer until the liquid has reduced by half—about 10 minutes. In a small bowl, stir together the milk, flour, poultry seasoning, salt, and pepper. Slowly whisk the milk mixture into the saucepan. Stir in the reserved chicken and onions. Remove the skillet from the heat and let cool for 10 minutes.

★ TOP AND BAKE THE PIE: Top the chicken mixture with the piecrust and cut slits to allow steam to escape. Bake until the crust is golden and the filling is bubbly—30 to 35 minutes. Let cool slightly and serve from the skillet.

NUTRITION INFORMATION PER SERVING—protein: 31 g; fat: 17 g; carbohydrate: 32 g; fiber: 4 g; sodium: 769 mg; cholesterol: 87 mg; calories: 402.

FLAKY PIECRUST

If you have the time to make piecrust from scratch, here's a recipe you may want to use for our Chicken Potpie as well as for any sweet filling.

1¹⁄₂ **cups all-purpose flour**

¹⁄₂ **teaspoon salt**

¹⁄₂ **cup vegetable shortening**

4 to 5 tablespoons ice water

MAKE THE CRUST: In a medium bowl, combine the flour and salt. Using a pastry blender or 2 knives, cut the shortening into the dry ingredients until the mixture resembles very coarse crumbs. Add the ice water, 1 tablespoon at a time, mixing lightly with a fork, until the pastry is moist enough to hold together in a flattened ball. Wrap the dough ball in waxed paper and refrigerate until chilled—about 30 minutes.

BAKE THE CRUST: Between 2 sheets of floured waxed paper, roll out the chilled pastry to an 11-inch round. Remove the top sheet of waxed paper and invert the crust over the filling. Remove the remaining sheet of waxed paper and trim excess pastry to fit the baking dish. Bake as directed in the third step of the Chicken Potpie recipe (opposite).

This is the ideal pantry dish—the only items you will likely need to purchase are the sausages and fresh cilantro. Serve with warmed flour tortillas folded into triangles to scoop up the hearty mixture. Alternatively, fill the tortillas with the pilaf, wrap them like burritos and accompany with salsa and a dollop of sour cream.

Mexican Rice, Beans, and Sausage

1¹/₂ cups long-grain white rice

1 small onion, chopped

1 13-ounce package Mexican-flavored
    smoked turkey-and-chicken sausages,
    cut diagonally into ¹/₄-inch-thick slices

1 tablespoon olive oil

1 14¹/₂-ounce can low-sodium
    chicken broth

1¹/₄ cups water

1 15-ounce can black beans, rinsed
    and drained

1 7-ounce can whole-kernel corn, drained

2 tablespoons chopped fresh
    cilantro leaves

★ **PREPARE THE RICE:** Preheat oven to 375°F. In a 2¹/₂-quart casserole or Dutch oven, combine the rice, onion, sausages, and olive oil, mixing to coat the rice completely with oil.

★ **HEAT THE BROTH MIXTURE:** In a 1-quart microwave-safe measuring cup in a microwave oven or in a saucepan over medium heat, bring the broth and water to a boil. Pour the broth mixture into the casserole and cover.

★ **BAKE THE RICE:** Bake the rice for 30 minutes. Stir in the black beans, corn, and cilantro. Cover and bake until all liquid is absorbed—15 to 20 more minutes. Serve hot.

Tip If fresh corn is in season, by all means, use it. Remove the kernels from the cob by standing it on its wide end and using a sharp knife to slice the kernels off.

NUTRITION INFORMATION PER SERVING—protein: 20 g; fat: 12 g; carbohydrate: 61 g; fiber: 7 g; sodium: 746 mg; cholesterol: 44 mg; calories: 430.

The combination of oranges and fennel is commonly seen on the Italian table. This makes a great company dish—present it on a large rimmed platter, garnished with fresh orange slices and feathery fennel fronds.

Orange-Fennel Chicken

6 large boneless, skinless chicken
   breast halves

1 teaspoon salt

1/4 teaspoon ground black pepper

4 tablespoons olive oil

2 tablespoons fresh lemon juice

2 large fennel bulbs, outer layers discarded

2 large navel oranges, peeled

1 medium onion

1 1/2 cups orange juice

1 teaspoon fennel seeds, crushed

★ **MARINATE THE CHICKEN:** On a plate, sprinkle the chicken with 1/2 teaspoon of the salt and the pepper. Drizzle with 2 tablespoons of the olive oil and the lemon juice. Set aside for 15 minutes to marinate, turning the chicken over a few times to coat.

★ **PREPARE THE VEGETABLES AND ORANGES:** Meanwhile, trim the tops off the fennel bulbs, reserving some of the green fronds for garnish. Cut the fennel bulbs, oranges, and onion crosswise into 1/4-inch slices.

★ **BROWN THE CHICKEN:** In a large nonstick skillet, heat 1 tablespoon olive oil over medium-high heat. Add the chicken and cook until well browned on both sides. Transfer the chicken to a clean plate and set aside.

★ **COOK AND SERVE:** Add the remaining 1 tablespoon olive oil to the skillet; add the fennel and onion. Sauté for 5 minutes. Add the orange juice, fennel seeds, and the remaining 1/2 teaspoon salt. Bring to a boil over high heat and simmer until the juice is reduced by half. Return the browned chicken and any juices to the skillet and top the chicken with the orange slices. Simmer until the chicken is cooked through. Chop some of the reserved fennel fronds and sprinkle over the chicken. Serve immediately.

NUTRITION INFORMATION PER SERVING — protein: 29 g; fat: 12 g; carbohydrate: 20 g; fiber: 2 g; sodium: 465 mg; cholesterol: 73 mg; calories: 303.

Lower-fat turkey kielbasa replaces the traditional ham or bacon in this side dish turned main course. Here, the potatoes and sausage are tossed in a flour-thickened dressing of cider vinegar, sugar, and black pepper, creating at once sour, sweet, and hot flavors.

Turkey Kielbasa with Warm Potato Salad

2 pounds potatoes, peeled

2 tablespoons vegetable oil

1 small onion, chopped

1 pound turkey kielbasa, sliced

1 tablespoon all-purpose flour

1/2 cup water

3 tablespoons cider vinegar

1 tablespoon sugar

1/4 teaspoon ground black pepper

3/4 cup frozen green peas, thawed

★ COOK THE POTATOES: Cut the potatoes crosswise into 1/4-inch-thick slices. Put the potatoes in a 3-quart saucepan, cover with water, and bring to a boil over high heat. Reduce the heat to low; cover and cook the potatoes just until tender—about 15 minutes. Drain the potatoes in a colander.

★ COOK AND SERVE: In the same saucepan, heat the oil over medium heat. Add the onion and kielbasa; cook for 3 to 5 minutes or until the onion softens. Stir in the flour until well mixed, then stir in the 1/2 cup water, vinegar, sugar, and pepper. Cook, stirring, until thickened and bubbly. Reduce the heat to low. Gently stir in the cooked potatoes and peas and simmer for 5 minutes. Remove from the heat and serve.

NUTRITION INFORMATION PER SERVING — protein: 17 g; fat: 15 g; carbohydrate: 46 g; fiber: 5 g; sodium: 596 mg; cholesterol: 50 mg; calories: 385.

A great casual company dish, this stovetop-to-table skillet supper features a sweet-and-spicy sauce that is rich enough to stand up to the intense smoky flavor of the sausage. A nice Syrah, with its smoky undertones and bold flavors of black fruits, brings out the best in this hearty combination.

Barbecued Smoked Sausage and Lima Beans

2 teaspoons olive oil

4 5-inch smoked turkey-and-duck
    sausages (10 to 12 ounces)

1 medium onion, chopped (about 1 cup)

2 10-ounce packages frozen lima beans
    (preferably large Fordhook beans)

1 14 1/2-ounce can stewed tomatoes

1/4 cup packed light brown sugar

1/4 cup cider vinegar

1 teaspoon dry mustard

1 teaspoon chili powder

1/2 teaspoon ground ginger

1/4 teaspoon salt

★ COOK THE SAUSAGES: In a heavy 9-inch skillet, heat the olive oil over medium heat. With a fork, pierce the sausages all over several times. Add the sausages and onion to the skillet and cook, turning the sausages and stirring the onion occasionally, until lightly browned—about 4 minutes.

★ COOK THE LIMAS: Add the limas, stewed tomatoes, brown sugar, vinegar, mustard, chili powder, ginger, and salt; cover and bring to a boil. Reduce the heat to low and cook, stirring occasionally, until the limas are tender—10 to 12 minutes.

★ TO SERVE: With tongs, lift the sausages and arrange them on top of the beans. Serve hot from the skillet.

NUTRITION INFORMATION PER SERVING – protein: 21 g; fat: 8 g; carbohydrate: 53 g; fiber: 15 g; sodium: 971 mg; cholesterol: 55 mg; calories: 357.

Aromatic spices—including coriander, the mix of spices in curry powder, and cloves—give depth to this colorful Indian-inspired dish. Serve it in soup bowls accompanied by warm naan or pita bread for scooping up every last drop of the fragrant broth.

Chicken-and-Apple Sausage Curry

1 teaspoon olive oil

4 5-inch chicken-and-apple sausages,
    (10 to 12 ounces), each cut into
    4 pieces

1 large yellow bell pepper, cut
    into 1-inch pieces

1 medium onion, chopped

2 teaspoons curry powder

1 1/2 teaspoons fresh or 1/2 teaspoon
    dried thyme leaves

1 teaspoon ground coriander

1/4 teaspoon salt

1/8 teaspoon ground cloves

1/8 teaspoon ground red pepper
    (optional)

1 pound sweet potatoes
    (about 3 medium), peeled and
    sliced into 1-inch-thick rounds

2 1/2 cups water

1/2 pound green beans, trimmed
    and halved

1 tablespoon all-purpose flour

4 sprigs fresh thyme (optional)

Naan or pita bread (optional)

★ **MAKE THE SAUSAGE MIXTURE:** In a heavy 4-quart Dutch oven or deep skillet, heat the olive oil over medium heat. Add the sausages, bell pepper, and onion; sauté until browned—about 4 minutes.

★ **COOK THE SPICES:** Add the curry powder, thyme, coriander, salt, cloves, and if desired, red pepper; cook, stirring, until the spices are fragrant—about 1 minute.

★ **COOK THE VEGETABLES:** Add the sweet potatoes and 2 cups of the water; cover and bring to a boil. Reduce the heat to low and cook for 8 minutes. Add the green beans; cover and cook the vegetables just until tender—5 to 8 minutes.

★ **THICKEN THE CURRY:** In a small bowl, stir the remaining 1/2 cup water into the flour until smooth. Stir into the sausage mixture and bring to a boil, stirring constantly, until thickened.

★ **TO SERVE:** Spoon into 4 soup bowls. Garnish each with a thyme sprig and accompany with naan, if desired.

NUTRITION INFORMATION PER SERVING WITHOUT NAAN—protein: 13 g; fat: 9 g; carbohydrates: 35 g; fiber: 8 g; sodium: 522 mg; cholesterol: 55 mg; calories: 268.

Use shaped pasta for this deeply satisfying dish; the nooks and crannies are perfect for cradling the sausage and chunky vegetables. It's an ideal meal to serve impromptu guests since it requires little preparation and less than 30 minutes cooking time. Serve it with a tossed green salad and crisp Italian bread.

Italian-Seasoned Turkey Sausage with Pasta and Vegetables

2 tablespoons olive oil

1 pound Italian-seasoned turkey sausages, casings removed

1 medium onion, thinly sliced

2 medium zucchini (about 3/4 pound), quartered lengthwise and cut into 1/2-inch chunks

4 cloves garlic, chopped

2 teaspoons dried oregano

3 cups water

1/4 teaspoon salt

2 1/2 cups rotelle or spiral-shaped pasta

3 cups firmly packed fresh spinach leaves

2 plum tomatoes, seeded and diced

★ COOK THE SAUSAGES AND ZUCCHINI: In a 4-quart saucepan, heat the olive oil over medium heat. Add the sausage meat and onion; cook until lightly browned, stirring to break up the sausages—5 to 7 minutes. Add the zucchini, garlic, and oregano; cook for 5 minutes. Transfer the sausage mixture to a medium bowl.

★ COOK THE PASTA AND SERVE: In the same saucepan, bring the water and salt to a boil over high heat. Add the pasta and cook for 10 to 12 minutes or until cooked through and most of the liquid is absorbed. Reduce the heat to low; return the sausage mixture to the saucepan and mix well. Stir in the spinach and plum tomatoes. Transfer to a large bowl and serve hot.

NUTRITION INFORMATION PER SERVING — protein: 26 g; fat: 17 g; carbohydrate: 50 g; fiber: 5 g; sodium: 626 mg; cholesterol: 61 mg; calories: 457.

Smoked chicken or turkey sausage infuses this classic hearty Italian soup with warmth. Accompany the soup with rich and satisfying Asiago cheese toasts.

Tuscan Bean Soup with Asiago Toasts

1 tablespoon vegetable oil

1 pound smoked turkey or chicken
   sausage, cut into 1/4-inch rounds

1 1/4 cups chopped fennel

1 1/4 cups chopped onion

1 clove garlic, finely chopped

2 14 1/2-ounce cans low-sodium
   chicken broth

1 14 1/2-ounce can diced tomatoes

1/4 teaspoon rubbed sage

1/4 teaspoon ground black pepper

1 19-ounce can cannellini beans with liquid

1/2 cup grated Asiago cheese

12 1/2-inch-thick diagonal slices baguette

★ **MAKE THE SOUP:** In a 6-quart stockpot, heat the oil over medium heat. Add the sausage and sauté until heated through—5 to 7 minutes. Remove the sausage and discard all but 1 tablespoon drippings from the pot. Add the fennel and onion to the pot; sauté until softened—about 10 minutes. Add the garlic and cook 1 minute. Stir in the chicken broth, tomatoes, sage, and pepper. Cook for 10 minutes. Add the cannellini beans with their liquid and the reserved sausage. Bring the mixture to a boil over medium-high heat and cook for 1 minute. Reduce the heat to low and simmer for 10 more minutes.

★ **MAKE THE ASIAGO TOASTS:** Heat the broiler. Mound 2 teaspoons Asiago cheese on each bread slice and place on a baking sheet. Broil until the cheese and bread are lightly toasted—1 to 2 minutes. Divide the soup among 6 servings bowls and serve with the toasts.

Tip This soup becomes more flavorful with time; make it a day in advance of serving, cover, and refrigerate. Bring it to room temperature and warm over moderate heat.

NUTRITION INFORMATION PER SERVING — protein: 33 g; fat: 16 g; carbohydrate: 65 g; fiber: 10 g; sodium: 1,361 mg; cholesterol: 68 mg; calories: 532.

The flavors of Thai cuisine infuse this soothing soup, a perfect choice for a hearty lunch or light dinner. Ginger, lemongrass, and chili paste flavor the delicate broth, while wheat noodles and white-meat chicken add substance.

Chicken and Mushroom Noodle Soup

8 cups low-sodium chicken broth

6 green onions, cut into 1-inch pieces, white bottoms separated

2 teaspoons chopped peeled fresh ginger

1 1½-inch piece fresh lemongrass, chopped or 1 tablespoon dried

1 pound boneless, skinless chicken breasts

½ pound assorted mushrooms (such as shiitake, oyster, or cremini), sliced

2 tablespoons low-sodium soy sauce

½-1 teaspoon Chinese chili paste

3½ ounces thin somen or ramen noodles, cooked and drained

2 ounces baby spinach

★ **POACH THE CHICKEN:** In a large stockpot, combine the broth, the white bottoms of the green onions, ginger, and lemongrass and bring to a boil. Add the chicken, reduce the heat to medium, and cook until the chicken is cooked through—about 20 minutes. Remove the chicken and skim the fat from the broth. Shred the chicken, cover with plastic wrap, and set aside.

★ **FINISH THE SOUP:** Strain the broth through cheesecloth or a very fine sieve and return to the stockpot. Add the mushrooms and green onion tops to the broth and bring to a boil over high heat. Reduce the heat to low and simmer for 10 minutes. Add the chicken back to the broth, stir in the soy sauce and chili paste, and simmer for 10 more minutes. Divide the noodles and spinach among 6 bowls and ladle the hot soup into the bowls. Serve immediately.

Tip *Lemongrass is now available in a refrigerated paste that can be substituted for fresh lemongrass. Tubes of the paste have a guide on the back for substituting it for fresh lemongrass.*

NUTRITION INFORMATION PER SERVING — protein: 23.3 g; fat: 4 g; carbohydrate: 11 g; fiber: 2.3 g; sodium: 466 mg; cholesterol: 53 mg; calories: 162.

There are undoubtedly as many versions of this beloved soup as there are mothers and fathers who make it. Ours is pretty straightforward; after all, you don't want to put anything fancy in this cold-weather standard. The leeks may be an unlikely addition, but they add nice flavor and texture.

Chicken Noodle Soup

1 $3^1/2$-pound whole chicken, rinsed and patted dry

16 cups (3 quarts) low-sodium chicken broth

6 carrots, peeled

4 stalks celery, trimmed

3 medium onions, peeled

5 whole black peppercorns

1 clove garlic, crushed with the side of a knife

10 sprigs fresh parsley

2 sprigs fresh thyme

1 bay leaf

2 tablespoons unsalted butter

4 leeks, tops and root ends removed, cleaned, and sliced $1/4$ inch thick

1 teaspoon salt

1 teaspoon ground black pepper

3 cups medium egg noodles (5 ounces)

★ **MAKE THE STOCK:** Place the chicken and chicken broth in a large stockpot and set it over medium heat. Roughly chop 2 carrots, 2 celery stalks, and 1 onion and add to the broth. Add the peppercorns, garlic, 2 sprigs of parsley, the thyme, the bay leaf, and enough water to just cover the chicken. Bring the broth to a boil, reduce the heat to low, and simmer until the chicken is very tender—about $1^1/4$ hours—skimming the surface periodically. Transfer the chicken to a large bowl. Strain the broth through a fine sieve into a large, clean bowl. Discard the vegetables and bay leaves. Rinse and dry the stockpot.

★ **MAKE THE SOUP:** Skim any fat from the broth. Slice the remaining carrots, celery, and onions into $1/4$-inch-thick pieces and set aside. Remove and discard the skin and bones from the chicken, cut the meat into $1/2$-inch pieces, and set aside. Chop the remaining parsley leaves. Melt the butter in the same stockpot over medium heat. Add the leeks and the sliced carrots, celery, and onions and cook until the onions are translucent—about 7 minutes. Add the chicken, the reserved broth, salt, and pepper. Bring to a boil; reduce heat and simmer the soup until the vegetables are tender—about 1 hour. Stir in the egg noodles and chopped parsley and cook until the noodles are tender—about 10 more minutes. Serve hot.

NUTRITION INFORMATION PER SERVING—protein: 25.9 g; fat: 6.6 g; carbohydrate: 17.6 g; fiber: 2.8 g; sodium: 314 mg; cholesterol: 86.6 mg; calories: 229.

The warmth of ground cumin and oregano and the heat of chili powder and fresh roasted jalapeños come together in this chowder inspired by the flavors of the Southwest. Red bell peppers and golden kernels of corn mingle with the pumpkin to create a delicious, autumnal soup.

Pumpkin and Chicken Chowder

2 red bell peppers

2 jalapeño peppers

2 tablespoons olive oil

1¹/₂ pounds boneless, skinless chicken breasts, diced

1 2-pound pumpkin, peeled, seeded, and cut into 1-inch chunks

3 leeks, white and light-green parts only, cleaned and sliced ¹/₄ inch thick

3 tablespoons all-purpose flour

2 teaspoons ground cumin

1 teaspoon chili powder

1 teaspoon salt

¹/₂ teaspoon ground black pepper

1 ear corn, husked and silked, kernels removed (about 1 cup)

3 14¹/₂-ounce cans low-sodium chicken broth

1 tablespoon chopped fresh oregano leaves

¹/₂ cup sour cream (optional)

★ ROAST THE PEPPERS: Preheat oven to broil. Place the bell peppers and jalapeños on a baking sheet and cook under the broiler, turning occasionally, until the skins blacken—about 10 minutes. Seal the charred peppers in a plastic bag for 10 to 12 minutes. Peel, stem, seed, and cut the peppers into ¹/₂-inch pieces. Set aside.

★ MAKE THE SOUP: In a large Dutch oven, heat the olive oil over medium-high heat. Add the chicken and sauté until lightly browned. With a slotted spoon, transfer the chicken to a bowl and keep warm. Add the pumpkin and leeks and sauté about 5 minutes. Stir in the flour, cumin, chili powder, salt, and pepper and cook, stirring, for 1 to 2 minutes. Add the corn, roasted peppers, the browned chicken and any juices, chicken broth, and oregano and bring to a boil. Reduce the heat to low and simmer until the leeks and pumpkin are tender—about 30 minutes. Garnish with sour cream, if desired; serve hot.

Tip *Use a stovetop-to-table Dutch oven, such as the colorful enamel-coated cast iron kind and make the soup the centerpiece on the table. Place two small bowls of sour cream on either side of it.*

NUTRITION INFORMATION PER SERVING WITH SOUR CREAM – protein: 11.4 g; fat: 8.1 g; carbohydrate: 10.7 g; fiber: 1.8 g; sodium: 207 mg; cholesterol: 32 mg; calories: 157.

Based on the classic New England one-dish meal that traditionally features bacon or ham and a whole chicken, this celebration of soothing winter vegetables—carrots, turnips, and cabbage—is the perfect foil for poultry- or pork-based sausages.

Chicken-and-Spinach Sausage Boiled Dinner

2 teaspoons butter

8 small white onions (about 3/4 pound), peeled

4 5-inch low-fat chicken-and-spinach sausages (10 to 12 ounces)

4 cups water

4 medium carrots (about 1/2 pound), peeled and halved

4 medium turnips (about 1/2 pound), peeled and halved

1/4 teaspoon salt

1 small cabbage (about 1 pound), quartered

1 tablespoon chopped fresh parsley leaves

★ **COOK THE SAUSAGES:** In a heavy 4-quart saucepan or Dutch oven, melt the butter over medium heat. Add the onions and sausages; cook, turning the sausages and onions occasionally until lightly browned—about 4 minutes. Transfer the sausages to a plate, leaving the onions in the saucepan.

★ **COOK THE VEGETABLES:** Add the water, carrots, turnips, and salt; cover and bring to a boil over high heat. Reduce the heat to low and cook 10 minutes. Add the cabbage and cook until the vegetables are just tender— 5 to 8 minutes.

★ **REHEAT THE SAUSAGES:** Return the sausages to the pan; making sure they are covered by broth. Cook, uncovered, just until the sausages are heated through (they will start to expand)—about 5 minutes. Do not overcook or the sausages will split.

★ **TO SERVE:** With a slotted spoon, transfer the sausages and vegetables to a serving platter and ladle the broth into a soup tureen; or divide the sausages, vegetables, and broth among 4 soup plates. Sprinkle with chopped parsley and serve immediately.

NUTRITION INFORMATION PER SERVING – protein: 15 g; fat: 6 g; carbohydrate: 24 g; fiber: 8 g; sodium: 554 mg; cholesterol: 55 mg; calories: 197.

A whole jalapeño heats up the tomatillo-based flavor paste in this green chili, made fragrant with cumin and coriander. Tortilla chips are a classic accompaniment and easy to make yourself: Spray fresh flour or corn tortillas with vegetable oil, stack them, cut them into wedges or strips, and bake on a nonstick baking sheet at 400°F for 5 to 7 minutes.

Chicken-Tomatillo Chili

1 11-ounce can tomatillos or 7 or 8 fresh tomatillos, husks removed, rinsed, and quartered

1 jalapeño pepper, halved and seeded

2 tablespoons vegetable oil

2 pounds boneless, skinless chicken thighs, cut into 1-inch pieces

1 medium onion, chopped (about 1 cup)

3 cloves garlic, minced

2 4$\frac{1}{2}$-ounce cans diced green chiles

2 teaspoons ground cumin

1 teaspoon ground coriander

2 14$\frac{1}{2}$-ounce cans low-sodium chicken broth

$\frac{1}{2}$ cup chopped fresh cilantro leaves

1 teaspoon salt

Tortilla chips or strips (optional)

★ **MAKE THE FLAVOR PASTE:** In a blender or food processor fitted with a metal blade, combine the tomatillos and jalapeño. Blend until thick and smooth—about 1 minute. Set aside.

★ **BROWN THE CHICKEN:** In a large Dutch oven, heat the oil over medium-high heat until hot but not smoking. Add the chicken and cook until browned—3 to 4 minutes. Remove and set aside.

★ **MAKE THE CHILI:** Add the onion to the Dutch oven and sauté until translucent—about 3 minutes. Add the garlic, sauté 1 minute, and then add the chicken, chiles, cumin, coriander, chicken broth, and the flavor paste. Bring to a boil and reduce the heat to low. Simmer, uncovered, for 45 minutes.

★ **TO SERVE:** Stir in the cilantro and salt. Serve the chili with tortilla chips, if desired.

NUTRITION INFORMATION PER SERVING WITHOUT TORTILLA CHIPS—protein: 32.2 g; fat: 17.3 g; carbohydrate: 9.6 g; fiber: 2.8 g; sodium: 541 mg; cholesterol: 105 mg; calories: 320.

The aromatic flavors of Provence perfume this crowd-pleasing stew, an ideal choice for a weekend gathering in which friends may come and go. Prepare it ahead and keep it warm on the stove, ready whenever you and your guests are.

Chicken Provençale

2 tablespoons olive oil

6 4-ounce boneless, skinless chicken thighs, each cut in half

2 medium onions, thinly sliced

1 medium fennel bulb, thinly sliced

6 cloves garlic, thinly sliced

1 28-ounce can whole tomatoes with thick tomato puree

1 14$^{1}/_{2}$-ounce can low-sodium chicken broth

2 teaspoons dried thyme

$^{1}/_{2}$ teaspoon salt

$^{1}/_{2}$ teaspoon ground black pepper

$^{1}/_{2}$ cup pitted ripe olives

$^{1}/_{2}$ cup dry red wine

Fresh thyme sprigs (optional)

★ BROWN THE CHICKEN: In a heavy 6-quart stockpot, heat 1 tablespoon of the olive oil over medium heat. Add the chicken and cook until the pieces are browned on all sides—about 5 minutes. Remove the chicken to a medium bowl and set aside.

★ COOK THE STEW: Add the remaining tablespoon olive oil, the onions, and fennel to the stockpot; sauté until golden—about 10 minutes. Add the garlic and sauté for 2 minutes. Return the browned chicken to the stockpot with the vegetables. Add the tomatoes with puree, chicken broth, dried thyme, salt, and pepper. Bring the stew to a boil over high heat. Reduce the heat to low; cover and cook for 45 minutes. Add the olives and red wine; cover and cook 15 more minutes, stirring occasionally.

★ TO SERVE: Ladle 2 pieces of chicken with some tomato-vegetable mixture into each of 6 soup plates. Garnish each with a sprig of thyme, if desired.

NUTRITION INFORMATION PER SERVING—protein: 25 g; fat: 13 g; carbohydrate: 12 g; fiber: 3 g; sodium: 786 mg; cholesterol: 97 mg; calories: 286.

Dry white wine replaces the traditional Burgundy in this version of the classic French country dish. Aromatic herbs and fresh vegetables are steeped in white wine to make a tenderizing marinade for the chicken, which then becomes a foundation for the sauce in the finished dish.

Coq au Vin Blanc

MARINADE

3 cups dry white wine

1 medium onion, chopped (about 1 cup)

1 small carrot, sliced

1 stalk celery, sliced

3 cloves garlic, chopped

2 tablespoons olive oil

1 to 2 tablespoons loosely packed fresh flat-leaf parsley

8 whole black peppercorns

1/2 teaspoon salt

6 pounds assorted bone-in chicken pieces (thighs, breasts, drumsticks)

COQ AU VIN

4 slices bacon, chopped

1 tablespoon olive oil

12 fresh or frozen small white onions, peeled

5 medium carrots, peeled and cut into 1-inch chunks (about 2 cups)

2 stalks celery, sliced (about 1 cup)

3 cloves garlic, chopped

1 shallot, chopped

1/4 cup unsifted all-purpose flour

3 cups low-sodium chicken broth

1 tablespoon balsamic vinegar

1 bay leaf

1 teaspoon chopped fresh thyme leaves

1/2 teaspoon salt

1/4 teaspoon ground black pepper

1 pound small red potatoes, scrubbed

★ MARINATE THE CHICKEN: In a 3-quart saucepan, combine the white wine, onion, carrot, celery, garlic, olive oil, parsley, peppercorns, and salt. Bring to a boil over medium-high heat. Reduce the heat to low and simmer for 5 minutes. Remove the pan from the heat and let the marinade cool to room temperature. In a large nonreactive container, arrange the chicken pieces and pour the cooled marinade over them. Cover and refrigerate at least 4 hours or overnight.

★ BROWN THE CHICKEN: Remove the chicken from the marinade and pat dry. Strain the marinade and reserve the liquid; discard the vegetables. In a 6-quart Dutch oven or heavy kettle, cook the bacon over medium heat until crisp. Using a slotted spoon, transfer the bacon to paper towels. Brown the chicken parts in the bacon drippings in the Dutch oven. Remove the chicken from the Dutch oven and discard all but 1 tablespoon drippings. Add the olive oil and white onions; sauté onions until lightly browned—8 to 10 minutes. Add the carrots, celery, garlic, and shallot; sauté 5 minutes longer.

★ **BRAISE THE CHICKEN:** In a medium bowl, stir together the reserved marinade liquid and the flour. Add the mixture to the Dutch oven and stir in the chicken broth, vinegar, bay leaf, thyme, salt, and pepper. Return the browned chicken and any juices to the pan and bring to a boil over medium-high heat, stirring frequently. Reduce the heat to low; cover and cook for 45 minutes. Add the potatoes and cook until fork-tender—about 20 more minutes. Remove and discard the bay leaf. Divide the stew evenly among 6 serving bowls. Garnish each serving with reserved chopped bacon.

NUTRITION INFORMATION PER SERVING — protein: 61 g; fat: 24 g; carbohydrate: 41 g; fiber: 5 g; sodium: 1,096 mg; cholesterol: 176 mg; calories: 708.

Named for the oval earthenware pot in which it is ideally baked, this version of the French specialty of slow-cooked white beans and meat—here we use duck—is streamlined so that it can be prepared in about 2 hours. Alternatively, prepare it a day or two ahead and slowly reheat before serving.

Long Island Duckling Cassoulet

1 1-pound package dried white beans

1/4 pound sliced bacon, chopped

1 pound boneless, skinless duckling breasts, cut into 2-inch pieces

3 cups water

2 14 1/2-ounce cans low-sodium chicken broth

3 medium onions, sliced

3 carrots, peeled and sliced 1/2 inch thick

1 stalk celery, chopped

3 cloves garlic, chopped

1 pound low-fat kielbasa, sliced into rounds

1 15-ounce can crushed tomatoes

2 teaspoons dried thyme

1/2 teaspoon cracked black pepper

1 cup fresh bread crumbs

★ **PREPARE THE BEANS:** Sort and soak the beans following the package directions. Drain and rinse.

★ **BROWN THE DUCKLING:** In an 8-quart Dutch oven, sauté the bacon over medium heat until browned. With a slotted spoon, transfer the bacon to a medium bowl. In the same pan with the bacon drippings, cook the duckling until well browned. Transfer to the bowl with the bacon; cover with plastic wrap and refrigerate.

★ **COOK THE BEANS:** In the same Dutch oven with drippings, combine the soaked beans, the water, broth, onions, 1 carrot, the celery, and garlic and bring to a boil over high heat. Reduce the heat to low; cover and simmer bean mixture for 1 hour.

★ **BAKE THE CASSOULET:** Preheat oven to 375°F. Stir the remaining 2 carrots, the browned duck breasts and bacon, kielbasa, tomatoes, thyme, and pepper into bean mixture. Sprinkle the bread crumbs over the top. Transfer to the oven and bake, uncovered, for 45 to 60 minutes or until a brown crust forms. Serve hot.

NUTRITION INFORMATION PER SERVING — protein: 38 g; fat: 26 g; carbohydrate: 48 g; fiber: 4 g; sodium: 1,240 mg; cholesterol: 94 mg; calories: 580.

Seafood

Thin slices of fresh lemon and pitted olives separate layers of potatoes and salmon in this pretty company's-coming dish, which is best baked in an attractive oven-to-table casserole so that guests can enjoy your handiwork.

Wild Salmon and Potato Casserole with Citrus-Herb Vinaigrette

SALMON AND POTATOES

1 pound new potatoes, scrubbed and cut into $1/4$-inch-thick slices

1 tablespoon olive oil

$1/2$ teaspoon salt

$1/4$ teaspoon ground black pepper

1 1-pound wild salmon fillet, skin removed

1 lemon, scrubbed and sliced into $1/4$-inch-thick rounds

12 pitted black olives, such as niçoise or picholine

VINAIGRETTE

$1/4$ cup olive oil

2 tablespoons fresh lemon juice

1 tablespoon fresh orange juice

$1/4$ teaspoon salt

$1/8$ teaspoon ground black pepper

2 tablespoons chopped fresh basil leaves

1 teaspoon fresh thyme leaves

★ ROAST THE POTATOES: Preheat oven to 425°F. In an 8½-by-11-inch casserole or baking dish, place the potatoes in a single later. Drizzle with the olive oil and sprinkle with $1/4$ teaspoon of the salt and $1/8$ teaspoon of the pepper. Roast for 15 minutes. Remove from oven.

★ ROAST THE SALMON: Sprinkle the salmon on both sides with the remaining $1/4$ teaspoon salt and remaining $1/8$ teaspoon pepper. Layer half the lemon slices over the potatoes. Lay the salmon fillet on top of the lemon slices and place the remaining lemon slices on top. Scatter the olives over. Reduce oven temperature to 250°F and bake the casserole until the salmon and potatoes are cooked through—about 40 minutes.

★ MAKE THE CITRUS VINAIGRETTE: In a small bowl, whisk the olive oil, lemon juice, orange juice, salt, and pepper. Stir in the basil and thyme and drizzle over the warm salmon. Serve immediately.

NUTRITION INFORMATION PER SERVING—protein: 18.5 g; fat: 14.9 g; carbohydrate: 37.4 g; fiber: 3.6 g; sodium: 394 mg; cholesterol: 41.6 mg; calories: 354.

Gumbo filé powder, the dried and ground leaves of the sassafras tree, gives this Cajun specialty its hallmark flavor and texture. Don't allow the stew to come to a boil after you've added the filé or its texture will become unappetizing. This recipe feeds a crowd, but it freezes well and gets better with time; don't hesitate to put leftovers in a rigid container and freeze. Tradition dictates serving gumbo over rice with a wedge of cornbread.

Seafood Gumbo

1 cup all-purpose flour

1 cup vegetable oil

6 stalks celery, diced (about 3 cups)

3 medium onions, diced (about 3 cups)

3 large green bell peppers, diced
   (about 3 cups)

7 cups low-sodium chicken broth

$1^1/_2$ pounds okra, cut into $^1/_2$-inch-thick
   slices (about 3 cups)

1 pound smoked ham, diced

$^1/_2$ pound crabmeat, picked over and
   shell pieces discarded

2 28-ounce cans crushed tomatoes

$^1/_2$ cup chopped fresh flat-leaf parsley

1 tablespoon fresh lemon juice

1 tablespoon sugar

1 teaspoon dried oregano

$^1/_2$ teaspoon dried thyme

$^1/_2$ teaspoon Old Bay seasoning

$^1/_2$ teaspoon salt

$^1/_4$ teaspoon ground red pepper

$^1/_4$ teaspoon ground black pepper

2 pounds fresh or frozen medium shrimp,
   peeled and deveined

$^1/_2$ teaspoon gumbo filé powder

9 cups cooked rice

Hot-pepper sauce, to taste

★ COOK THE ROUX AND VEGETABLES: In a 12-quart heavy kettle or Dutch oven, heat the flour and oil over medium-low heat. Cook, stirring frequently, until the flour browns to a dark, mahogany color, being careful not to let it burn—40 to 50 minutes. Stir in the celery, onions, and bell peppers. Cook, stirring occasionally, until the vegetables are soft—about 30 minutes.

★ COOK AND SERVE: Add the chicken broth, okra, ham, and crabmeat; cook 40 more minutes. Stir in the tomatoes, parsley, lemon juice, sugar, oregano, thyme, Old Bay seasoning, salt, red pepper, and black pepper. Cook for 30 minutes. Stir in the shrimp and filé powder; cook until the shrimp are opaque throughout—about 15 more minutes. Serve warm over rice with hot-pepper sauce or freeze for up to 2 months.

Tip Be sure to add the filé powder no sooner than 15 minutes before the end of cooking time. If you add it to the pot too early, the gumbo becomes unpleasantly thick.

NUTRITION INFORMATION PER SERVING WITH $^1/_2$ CUP RICE—protein: 39 g; fat: 20 g; carbohydrate: 42 g; fiber: 3 g; sodium: 788 mg; cholesterol: 156 mg; calories: 512.

A garlic-butter sauce enriches this twist on the traditional seaside dish of shellfish and potatoes. The combination makes for a beautiful—and colorful—presentation. Radishes, carrots, red potatoes, and sweet potatoes are nestled among lobster, mussels, and clams; spoon it all onto a large rimmed platter and place in the center of the table so you and your guest (this serves only two) can serve yourselves. Or ladle it into individual shallow rimmed bowls.

Shore Dinner with Root Vegetables

4 small red potatoes (about ¼ pound), scrubbed and peeled

4 large radishes (about ¼ pound)

4 small carrots (about ¼ pound)

4 small onions (about ¼ pound), peeled

1 medium sweet potato (about ¼ pound), peeled and quartered

¼ teaspoon salt

⅛ teaspoon ground black pepper

4 3-ounce frozen slipper lobster tails, thawed

6 littleneck clams, scrubbed

6 mussels, scrubbed and beards removed

2 tablespoons olive oil

3 large cloves garlic, thinly sliced lengthwise

2 tablespoons butter

1 tablespoon finely chopped fresh parsley leaves

6 lemon wedges

★ STEAM THE VEGETABLES AND SEAFOOD: Into an 8-quart stockpot, place a wire rack and add 1½ inches water. Place the red potatoes and radishes on the rack. Cover and bring the water to a boil over high heat; reduce the heat to low and steam the vegetables for 5 minutes. Add the carrots, onions, sweet potato, salt, and pepper; stir to combine. Steam for 5 minutes. Add the lobster tails, clams, and mussels; steam until the vegetables are tender and the clams and mussels have opened—10 to 12 more minutes. Check the water level and add more if necessary. If using an automatic steamer, follow directions.

★ MAKE THE GARLIC SAUCE: Meanwhile, in a small skillet, heat the olive oil over medium heat. Add the garlic and sauté just until the edges start to brown; remove from the heat and stir in the butter.

★ TO SERVE: With tongs, remove the clams and mussels to a serving bowl, discarding any with unopened shells. Remove the vegetables and lobster tails to the bowl. Drizzle the garlic sauce over all. Sprinkle with parsley and serve with lemon wedges.

NUTRITION INFORMATION PER SERVING—protein: 46 g; fat: 29 g; carbohydrate: 42 g; fiber: 5 g; sodium: 1,037 mg; cholesterol: 191 mg; calories: 614.

This sunny orange stew gets its flavor and color from tomatoes and saffron, with a bit of cream stirred in at the end. Monkfish, sometimes known as poor man's lobster, is just as sweet and tender as the aforementioned shellfish.

Stewed Monkfish

4 tablespoons olive oil

3 tablespoons chopped garlic

3 tablespoon chopped shallots

6 7-ounce monkfish fillets

6 cups diced plum tomatoes
   (about 15 tomatoes)

2 tablespoons tomato paste

1/8 teaspoon saffron threads

1/2 teaspoon salt

1/2 teaspoon ground black pepper

1/3 cup Cognac or brandy

1/4 cup heavy cream

1 tablespoon finely chopped fresh
   parsley leaves

★ MAKE THE STEW: In a 6-quart stockpot, heat 2 tablespoons of the olive oil over high heat. Sauté the garlic and shallots, remove from the pot, and set aside. Wipe the pot with a paper towel and heat the remaining 2 tablespoons olive oil. Sauté the monkfish in batches until lightly browned and remove. Wipe the pot clean again and add the plum tomatoes, tomato paste, saffron, salt, and pepper to the stockpot; stir until well blended. Add the Cognac and return the garlic, shallots, and browned monkfish to the stockpot. Cover and cook until monkfish is cooked through—4 to 6 minutes. Gently stir in the cream and parsley. Serve immediately.

NUTRITION INFORMATION PER SERVING — protein: 40.2 g; fat: 17.2 g; carbohydrate: 15 g; fiber: 2.5 g; sodium: 664 mg; cholesterol: 77 mg; calories: 402.

This frittata makes a fine brunch, lunch, or dinner offering. Serve it on a brunch buffet with a fresh fruit salad and spicy link sausages, for lunch with a tangy arugula salad, or for dinner with a fresh beet salad and peasant bread.

Salmon and Goat Cheese Frittata

2 tablespoons vegetable oil

2 cups peeled, shredded potatoes
   (about 1¹/₂ large)

4 large eggs

4 large egg whites

1 tablespoon chopped fresh dill

¹/₂ teaspoon ground black pepper

¹/₄ teaspoon salt

4 ounces smoked salmon, cut into
   ¹/₂-inch pieces

6 ounces goat cheese, crumbled

★ COOK THE POTATOES: Preheat oven to 500°F. In a 10-inch nonstick, ovenproof skillet, heat the oil over medium-high heat. Add the potatoes and sauté until golden brown—about 10 minutes.

★ COOK THE FRITTATA: In a large bowl, beat the eggs, egg whites, dill, pepper, and salt. Stir in the smoked salmon. Pour the egg mixture over the potatoes and sprinkle the goat cheese over the top; reduce the heat to medium. Cook until the edges are set and the bottom is lightly browned—about 5 minutes. Place the pan in the oven and bake until the center of the frittata is set and the top is golden brown—about 3 minutes. Cut into 6 slices and serve immediately or reduce the oven temperature to 200°F if keeping warm.

NUTRITION INFORMATION PER SERVING—protein: 15.9 g; fat: 14.7 g; carbohydrate: 7.8 g; fiber: .7 g; sodium: 421 mg; cholesterol: 159 mg; calories: 229.

Ask any New Englander which is their favorite chowder and they'll be hard pressed to give you an answer. Here is a combination of the two northeastern classics.

Clam-and-Corn Chowder

4 slices bacon, coarsely chopped

1 medium onion, chopped (about 1 cup)

2 cups water

1 pound russet potatoes, peeled and cubed

1/2 teaspoon salt

1/4 teaspoon ground black pepper

3 6½-ounce cans chopped clams, drained with juice reserved

2 cups milk

1/4 cup all-purpose flour

1½ cups fresh or frozen whole-kernel corn

1 cup half-and-half

1 tablespoon chopped fresh parsley leaves

★ COOK THE BACON AND ONION: In a 5-quart Dutch oven or heavy stockpot, cook the bacon over medium heat until crisp and browned. Using a slotted spoon, transfer the bacon to a paper towel to drain. Discard all but 1 tablespoon drippings from the pot. Add the onion to the drippings and cook, stirring occasionally, until softened—2 to 3 minutes.

★ COOK THE SOUP: Add the water to the pot, stirring to loosen the browned bits on the bottom. Add the potatoes, salt, pepper, and reserved clam juice; stir and cover. Bring to a boil over high heat. Reduce the heat to low and cook until the potatoes are fork-tender—about 10 minutes.

★ FINISH THE SOUP: In a small bowl, combine the milk and flour. Add to the pot and stir. Return to a boil, stirring constantly, until the chowder has thickened. Add the corn and half-and-half and cook for 5 minutes. Add the reserved clams and cook just until the clams are heated through.

★ SERVE THE SOUP: Stir in the parsley and the reserved bacon. Divide among 6 soup bowls and serve.

NUTRITION INFORMATION PER SERVING—protein: 22 g; fat: 11 g; carbohydrate: 43 g; fiber: 4 g; sodium: 461 mg; cholesterol: 62 mg; calories: 354.

This somewhat refined version of the popular seafood restaurant offering features buttery fingerling potatoes and smoky bacon or pancetta. A hint of Asian chili paste adds color and heat.

Dungeness Crab and Mussel Chowder

14 ounces fingerling potatoes, scrubbed and cut into 1/4-inch-thick rounds

1/4 cup olive oil

1/4 pound sliced bacon or pancetta, cut into 1/4-inch pieces (about 1/2 cup)

3 tablespoons finely chopped garlic

3 tablespoons finely chopped shallots

1 tablespoon fresh thyme leaves

1 teaspoon grated lemon zest

1/2 teaspoon Asian chili paste, such as Sambal Oelek

3 tablespoons all-purpose flour

1 750-ml bottle pinot gris wine (about 3 cups)

1 1/2 pounds mussels, scrubbed and beards removed

2 cups coarsely chopped leeks

1/2 cup heavy cream

3/4 teaspoon salt

1/4 teaspoon ground black pepper

1 pound Dungeness crabmeat, picked over and shells discarded

★ PARBOIL THE POTATOES: Place the potatoes in a large nonreactive saucepan. Cover with about 2 inches cold water and bring to a boil over high heat. Reduce the heat to medium and cook until the potatoes just begin to soften—about 5 minutes. Drain the potatoes and set aside.

★ MAKE THE CHOWDER: In the same saucepan, heat the olive oil over medium heat. Add the bacon, garlic, shallots, thyme, lemon zest, and chili paste and cook, stirring frequently, until the shallots and garlic are softened and the bacon is lightly browned—about 6 minutes. Gradually add the flour, stirring well.

★ ADD THE WINE AND MUSSELS: Stir in the wine, blending it with the flour mixture. Stir in the mussels. Cover and bring to a boil. With a slotted spoon, remove the mussels as they open to a large bowl, discarding any with unopened shells. Cover and set aside. After all the mussels are cooked, reduce the heat to medium-low.

★ FINISH THE CHOWDER: Add the potatoes and leeks to the saucepan, cover, and simmer until tender—20 to 25 minutes. Remove from the heat and stir in the cream, salt, and pepper. Gently fold in the crabmeat and the cooked mussels. Serve immediately in warmed soup bowls.

NUTRITION INFORMATION PER SERVING – protein: 24.2 g; fat: 18.4 g; carbohydrate: 20 g; fiber: 2.3 g; sodium: 786 mg; cholesterol: 80 mg; calories: 387.

This elegant soup is the very definition of simplicity. Fresh fennel and fennel seeds infuse the broth with their hallmark delicate licorice flavor, a perfect match for sweet, succulent lobster meat.

Lobster-Fennel Soup

1 tablespoon olive oil

2 fennel bulbs, chopped

1½ teaspoons crushed fennel seeds

1 14½-ounce can low-sodium
    chicken broth

1½ cups water

½ cup cooked lobster meat

★ MAKE THE SOUP: In a large saucepan, heat the olive oil over medium heat. Add the fennel and fennel seeds and cook for 2 minutes. Add the chicken broth and water and bring to a boil. Reduce the heat to low; cover and simmer until the fennel is tender—about 25 minutes. Strain the broth, reserving the cooked fennel. Divide the broth between 2 serving bowls and add 3 tablespoons of the reserved fennel and the lobster meat. Serve immediately.

Tip Double this recipe to make a lovely hors d'oeuvres served in espresso or cordial glasses and garnished with a few fennel fronds.

NUTRITION INFORMATION PER SERVING—protein: 7 g; fat: 9.2 g; carbohydrate: 18.7 g; fiber: 10.6 g; sodium: 237 mg; cholesterol: 11 mg; calories: 165.

This may just be the easiest dish to make on your holiday menu. If you are shucking the oysters yourself, catch every drop of their flavorful liquor by working over a large bowl. Run the oyster liquor through a fine sieve or cheesecloth to remove any sand and grit.

Holiday Oyster Stew

3 tablespoons unsalted butter

2 shallots, minced

1 medium yellow onion, minced

1/2 cup minced celery

4 cups half-and-half

4 cups whole milk

1/4 teaspoon ground red pepper

1 teaspoon salt

1 teaspoon cracked black pepper

2 pints freshly shucked oysters, liquor reserved

2 tablespoons 1-inch-long pieces chives (optional)

★ **MAKE THE SOUP:** In a large saucepan, melt the butter over medium heat. Sauté the shallots, onion, and celery until soft—about 5 minutes. Stir in the half-and-half, milk, red pepper, salt, and cracked black pepper. Heat to just under a boil. Add the oysters and their liquor. Simmer just until the oysters begin to curl on the edges—about 5 minutes. Ladle the stew into soup bowls and sprinkle with chives, if desired.

NUTRITION INFORMATION PER SERVING—protein: 16.8 g; fat: 25.4 g; carbohydrate: 18.4 g; fiber: .6 g; sodium: 645 mg; cholesterol: 138 mg; calories: 367.

A little sautéing, a bit of stirring, and just 20 minutes baking results in this satisfying vegetarian dish inspired by the flavors of Indian cuisine. Plump golden raisins stud the curry-and-coriander-flavored rice and squash mixture.

Curried Butternut Squash and Rice Casserole

2 tablespoons vegetable oil

1 medium onion, chopped (about 1 cup)

1 shallot, chopped

1 tablespoon curry powder

1/2 teaspoon ground coriander

1 teaspoon salt

1/4 teaspoon ground black pepper

2 cups low-sodium vegetable broth

1 14-ounce can low-fat coconut milk
  (not cream of coconut)

1 11/2-pound butternut squash, peeled,
  halved, seeded, and cut into
  1/2-inch cubes (about 21/2 cups)

11/2 cups basmati rice

1/4 cup sliced almonds

1/4 cup golden raisins

★ COOK THE ONION AND SPICES: Preheat oven to 375°F. In a 4-quart shallow Dutch oven, heat the oil over medium heat. Add the onion, shallot, curry powder, coriander, salt, and pepper. Sauté the until onion has softened—5 to 7 minutes.

★ FINISH THE CASSEROLE AND BAKE: Stir in the broth and coconut milk. Bring the mixture to a boil over high heat. Cook for 1 minute. Remove the pan from the heat and stir in the squash, rice, almonds, and raisins. Cover tightly and place in the oven. Bake for 20 minutes. Carefully remove the cover and bake for 10 more minutes, until the rice and squash are tender. Serve immediately.

NUTRITION INFORMATION PER SERVING — protein: 6 g; fat: 7 g; carbohydrate: 57 g; fiber: 5 g; sodium: 567 mg; cholesterol: 4 mg; calories: 310.

This version of the popular Greek spanakopita is an ideal make-ahead dish; it can be assembled and frozen, then baked from the frozen state about 10 minutes longer than suggested in the fourth step. Purists may want to make their own phyllo, but the frozen variety works beautifully here.

Spinach-and-Cheese Pie

1 tablespoon vegetable oil

1 medium onion, chopped (about 1 cup)

2 10-ounce packages frozen chopped
    spinach, thawed and pressed until
    liquid has been extracted

1 15-ounce container part-skim
    ricotta cheese

1/2 pound feta cheese, crumbled

1/4 cup grated Parmesan cheese

3 large eggs

2 tablespoons chopped fresh
    parsley leaves

1 1/2 teaspoons dried oregano

1/8 teaspoon freshly grated nutmeg

13 12-by-17-inch frozen phyllo sheets,
    thawed

1/4 cup olive oil

2 tablespoons unseasoned bread crumbs

★ COOK THE ONION AND SPINACH: Heat the vegetable oil in a large skillet over medium heat. Add the onion and sauté until softened—5 to 7 minutes. Add the spinach and cook until all of the liquid has evaporated and the mixture is dry—about 5 minutes. Remove the skillet from the heat and let the mixture cool to room temperature.

★ MAKE THE FILLING: Preheat oven to 350°F. Grease a baking sheet (preferably a dark nonstick one) and set aside. In a large bowl, combine the ricotta, feta, and Parmesan cheeses. Stir in the eggs, parsley, oregano, and nutmeg. Add the onion-spinach mixture and combine. Set the filling aside.

★ ASSEMBLE THE PIE: Place the thawed phyllo sheets between 2 pieces of waxed paper, then cover the waxed paper with a clean, damp kitchen towel. (Since phyllo dough dries out very quickly, be sure to replace the damp towel each time you remove a sheet of phyllo and try to work as quickly as possible.) Remove one phyllo sheet and lay it on a work surface. Brush the sheet with olive oil and sprinkle lightly with bread crumbs. Repeat with 8 more sheets, placing each new one at an angle, like the petals of a flower, to form a circle. Spoon the reserved filling into the center of the sheets and pull the corners up around the filling. Brush the remaining 4 sheets of phyllo with olive oil and layer over the pie. Tuck the edges underneath to seal. Using a large spatula, transfer the pie to the prepared baking sheet or if freezing, wrap well in plastic and freeze..

★ BAKE AND SERVE: Brush the top of the pie with olive oil and bake until the filling feels firm to the touch and the dough is golden brown—45 to 55 minutes. Transfer the pie to a wire rack and let cool for at least 15 minutes before serving.

NUTRITION INFORMATION PER SERVING – protein: 17 g; fat: 22 g; carbohydrate: 14 g; fiber: 2 g; sodium: 549 mg; cholesterol: 121 mg; calories: 306.

Pimentón is a spicy, smoked paprika from Spain. Don't be alarmed at the amount of olive oil called for. It's used to "poach" the potatoes and most is drained away.

Tortilla Española

¾ **cup olive oil**

1½ **pounds Yukon Gold potatoes, peeled and thinly sliced**

2 **cups sliced yellow onions**

1½ **teaspoons salt**

6 **eggs**

1 **teaspoon** *pimentón*

½ **teaspoon freshly ground black pepper**

★ **PREPARE THE VEGETABLES:** Heat the olive oil in a 10-inch nonstick skillet over medium-low heat. Add the potatoes and cook, turning frequently, for 10 minutes. Stir in the onions and ½ teaspoon of the salt. Continue to cook for 25 more minutes until the vegetables are tender. Drain off the oil, reserving 2 tablespoons, and transfer the vegetables and reserved oil to separate bowls. Wipe the skillet clean.

★ **PREPARE THE TORTILLA:** In a large bowl, beat the eggs, *pimentón*, remaining 1 teaspoon salt, and the pepper. Stir in the cooked vegetables.

★ **COOK THE TORTILLA:** Heat 1 tablespoon of the reserved olive oil in the same skillet over medium-low heat. Pour the egg mixture into the skillet. Cook until just set—5 to 7 minutes. Loosen the sides with a spatula, place a heat-proof plate face down over the skillet, and invert the tortilla. Heat the remaining 1 tablespoon reserved olive oil in the skillet over low heat. Slide in the tortilla, cooked side up. Cook for 3 more minutes. Slide the tortilla onto a serving plate. Cool slightly before serving.

NUTRITION INFORMATION PER SERVING — protein: 9 g; fat: 19 g; carbohydrate: 25 g; sodium: 670 mg; cholesterol: 210 mg; calories: 300.

Asiago and provolone cheeses flavor this beautiful dish, which when sliced, displays colorful layers of spinach and tomatoes between fluffy eggs.

Two-Cheese Vegetable Strata

3 tablespoons olive oil

1 medium fennel bulb, trimmed and chopped

1 medium onion, thinly sliced

3 cloves garlic, sliced

1 14½-ounce can diced tomatoes

1 tablespoon Dijon mustard

8 cups coarsely chopped spinach

¼ teaspoon dried oregano

¼ teaspoon salt

¼ teaspoon ground black pepper

1 tablespoon butter

12 slices firm white bread, crusts removed

⅓ pound grated Asiago cheese

⅓ pound shredded provolone cheese

3 cups milk

6 large eggs

★ SAUTÉ THE VEGETABLES: In a 12-inch, straight-sided oven-proof skillet (with 2-inch-deep sides), heat the olive oil over medium heat. Add the fennel and onion and sauté for 10 minutes. Add the garlic and cook 1 more minute. Stir in the tomatoes and mustard; cook until the tomatoes soften—10 to 12 minutes. Stir in the spinach, oregano, salt, and pepper; cook 1 minute more. Transfer the mixture to a bowl and let cool for 10 minutes. Rinse and dry the skillet. Grease the skillet with the butter.

★ ASSEMBLE THE STRATA: Arrange half of the bread, overlapping if necessary, in the bottom of the prepared skillet. Top with half of the vegetable mixture, half of the Asiago cheese, and half of the provolone cheese. Make another layer with the remaining bread, vegetables, and cheeses.

★ ADD THE EGG MIXTURE AND CHILL: In a large bowl, lightly beat together the milk and eggs. Pour over the vegetable-and-cheese mixture (the filling will reach halfway up the sides). Cover the skillet tightly with plastic wrap and refrigerate overnight.

★ BAKE AND SERVE: When ready to serve, preheat oven to 350°F. Bake the strata, uncovered, until the center appears set—40 to 50 minutes. Serve immediately.

NUTRITION INFORMATION PER SERVING—protein: 16 g; fat: 16 g; carbohydrate: 23 g; fiber: 3 g; sodium: 572 g; cholesterol: 130 mg; calories: 298.

The speed with which you can put this crowd-pleaser together relies on good-quality purchased marinara. With just a quick sauté of mushrooms, onion, and peppers, the rest is easy; assemble the ingredients in layers and bake.

Zesty Vegetable Lasagna

2¹/₂ cups ricotta cheese

1 cup grated Pecorino Romano cheese

3 cloves garlic, finely chopped

1 tablespoon each dried oregano and
    dried basil

1 large egg

1 teaspoon each salt, pepper, and crushed
    red pepper

2 tablespoons extra-virgin olive oil

1 pound cremini mushrooms,
    roughly chopped

2 each red and yellow bell peppers, sliced
    into ¹/₄-inch-thick strips

1 large onion, sliced ¹/₄-inch thick

12 ounces baby spinach

4¹/₂ cups marinara sauce

1 pound no-boil lasagna noodles

1¹/₂ pounds fresh mozzarella cheese,
    sliced ¹/₄-inch thick

★ **MAKE THE FILLINGS:** In a large bowl, stir together the ricotta and Pecorino Romano cheeses, the garlic, herbs, egg, ¹/₂ teaspoon each salt and pepper, and the crushed red pepper. Heat 1 tablespoon of the olive oil in a large skillet over medium-high heat. Add the mushrooms and sauté until golden—about 3 minutes. Add the remaining 1 tablespoon olive oil, the bell peppers, and onion and cook until slightly softened—about 4 more minutes. Add the spinach and the remaining ¹/₂ teaspoon each salt and black pepper. Cook, stirring, until the spinach is wilted and tender—about 2 minutes. Set aside.

★ **ASSEMBLE AND BAKE THE LASAGNA:** Preheat oven to 350°F. Pour 1¹/₂ cups of the marinara sauce into a deep-dish 9-by-13-by-2-inch lasagna pan. Layer 5 lasagna noodles over the sauce. Top with half of the cooked vegetables and a third of the mozzarella. Layer with 5 more noodles and spread half the ricotta mixture over the noodles. Top with 1 cup of sauce and add another layer of noodles. Add the remaining vegetables, another third of the mozzarella, and a layer of noodles. Spread on the remaining ricotta mixture, 1 cup of sauce, and the last layer of noodles. Add the remaining sauce and mozzarella. Cover with aluminum foil and bake until bubbly—about 1 hour and 20 minutes. Let the lasagna cool slightly before serving.

NUTRITION INFORMATION PER SERVING — protein: 22.6 g; fat: 20.2 g; carbohydrate: 41.8 g; fiber: 4.2 g; sodium: 853 mg; cholesterol: 67 mg; calories: 454.

Soothing buttermilk tames the combination of Gorgonzola—an Italian blue cheese with a bite—and peppery arugula in this easy pasta dish. Serve it with a simple salad and Italian bread.

Gorgonzola-Buttermilk Pasta with Arugula

1 tablespoon plus ¼ teaspoon salt

8 ounces penne pasta

4 ounces Gorgonzola, crumbled

½ cup buttermilk

2 tablespoons chopped fresh
    flat-leaf parsley

¼ teaspoon coarsely ground
    black pepper

2 cups loosely packed fresh arugula,
    rinsed, dried, and torn

2 tablespoons pine nuts, toasted

★ MAKE THE PASTA: In a large pot over high heat, bring 4 quarts water to a boil. Add 1 tablespoon of the salt and stir in the pasta until the water boils again. Continue to cook for 10 to 12 minutes, until done. Remove from the heat and drain. Place in a large pasta bowl and set aside.

★ DRESS THE PASTA: In a small bowl, stir together the Gorgonzola, buttermilk, parsley, remaining ¼ teaspoon salt, and the pepper. Pour over the hot cooked pasta and toss to coat evenly.

★ SERVE THE PASTA: Add the arugula to the pasta, toss well, top with the pine nuts, and serve immediately.

> **Tip** *This pasta sauce makes an excellent dressing for a mixed green salad with the addition of 2 teaspoons of good-quality mayonnaise.*

NUTRITION INFORMATION PER SERVING — protein: 14 g; fat: 11 g; carbohydrate: 28.6 g; fiber: 4.4 g; sodium: 656 g; cholesterol: 26 g; calories: 261.

Fragrant with ginger, curry powder, and cumin, this colorful vegetarian preparation features the flavors of Thai cuisine. Coconut milk forms the base for gently browned tofu, sugar snap peas, and sweet red peppers.

Curried Tofu

1 14¹/₂- to 16-ounce package extra-firm tofu, drained, patted dry, and cut into 1¹/₂-inch cubes

1 tablespoon cornstarch

1 tablespoon peanut or corn oil

1 bunch green onions, chopped

3 tablespoons chopped peeled fresh ginger

4 teaspoons curry powder

1 teaspoon ground cumin

1 teaspoon grated lime zest

³/₄ teaspoon salt

¹/₄ teaspoon cracked black pepper

1¹/₂ pounds small red potatoes, scrubbed and halved

3 cups water

1 14-ounce can low-fat coconut milk (not cream of coconut)

¹/₂ pound sugar-snap pea pods, strings removed

1 large red bell pepper, cut into 1-inch squares

★ **BROWN THE TOFU:** In a large plastic bag, combine the tofu cubes and cornstarch. Shake until all the cornstarch adheres to the cubes. In a heavy 6-quart saucepot, heat the oil over medium heat. Add the tofu cubes and sauté until lightly browned on all sides—about 5 minutes.

★ **SEASON THE TOFU:** Stir in half of the green onions, the ginger, curry powder, cumin, lime zest, salt, and pepper; sauté 1 more minute.

★ **COOK AND SERVE:** Add the potatoes, water, and coconut milk to the curry. Bring to a boil over high heat, stirring constantly. Reduce the heat to low; cover and cook until the potatoes are just tender—about 20 minutes. Add the peas and bell pepper to the curry; bring to a boil over low heat, stirring occasionally. Serve hot.

Tip For a nonvegetarian variation of this dish, substitute two chicken breasts for the tofu. Cut the chicken into 1¹/₂-inch pieces.

NUTRITION INFORMATION PER SERVING BASED ON 14¹/₂ OUNCES OF TOFU — protein: 9 g; fat: 12 g; carbohydrate: 29 g; fiber: 5 g; sodium: 222 mg; cholesterol: 0; calories: 270.

When the first delicate stems of asparagus and tender shoots of green onions begin to appear in the spring, this is the dish to make—for any meal. Be sure to beat the eggs well for a gloriously fluffy frittata.

Asparagus Frittata

½ **pound wild or pencil-thin asparagus stalks, sliced diagonally into 2-inch pieces**

3 teaspoons olive oil

3 green onions, sliced

8 large eggs

3 tablespoons half-and-half

¼ **teaspoon salt**

¼ **teaspoon ground black pepper**

★ **COOK THE ASPARAGUS:** In a heavy 9-inch skillet, bring 2 inches of water to a boil over high heat. Add the asparagus and cook until just tender— 2 to 3 minutes. Drain the asparagus and place in a small bowl.

★ **COOK THE GREEN ONIONS:** Reduce the heat to medium and return the skillet to the heat until dry. Add 1 teaspoon of the olive oil and the green onions. Sauté the onions until softened. Remove the onions to the bowl with the asparagus. Heat the remaining 2 teaspoons olive oil in the skillet.

★ **MAKE THE EGG MIXTURE:** Meanwhile, beat the eggs until frothy. Add the half-and-half, salt, and pepper and beat until well combined. Fold in the asparagus and green onions.

★ **COOK THE FRITTATA:** Pour the mixture into the hot skillet. Cover and cook over medium heat until the frittata is set and most of the top surface looks dry—about 20 minutes.

★ **TO SERVE:** Run a knife around the side of the skillet to loosen the frittata and invert it onto a serving plate. Remove the skillet and cut the frittata into 8 wedges.

NUTRITION INFORMATION PER SERVING—protein: 7 g; fat: 7 g; carbohydrate: 2 g; fiber: .5 g; sodium: 133 mg; cholesterol: 214 mg; calories: 104.

Traditionally made with spinach, this take on the classic brunch offering features a red-stemmed variety of kale for a colorful alternative. Be sure to plunge the kale into a large bowl of water to wash away any dirt that may still be clinging to its leaves. Serve this for brunch or lunch with a salad lightly dressed with olive oil and lemon.

Kale and Cheese Frittata

1 pound 'Russian Red' kale

3 tablespoons butter

8 large eggs

1 cup half-and-half

1/2 teaspoon ground nutmeg

1/4 teaspoon salt

1/8 teaspoon ground black pepper

1/3 cup pine nuts

1/4 pound thinly sliced Swiss cheese, cut into strips

★ PREPARE THE KALE: Preheat oven to 350°F. Trim off and discard the kale stems. Stack a handful of leaves and cut them lengthwise into 1/2-inch-wide strips, then cut crosswise into 1-inch pieces. Set the leaves aside. Repeat to cut the remaining leaves.

★ SAUTÉ THE KALE: In a 9-inch ovenproof skillet, melt 1 tablespoon of the butter over medium heat. Add the kale and sauté just until tender. Remove from the heat.

★ BEAT THE EGGS: In a large bowl, beat the eggs, half-and-half, nutmeg, salt, and pepper. Stir in the sautéed kale.

★ COOK THE FRITTATA: In the same skillet, melt 1 tablespoon butter over medium heat. Add the pine nuts and sauté until golden; stir into the egg mixture. Add the remaining 1 tablespoon butter to the skillet and melt over medium heat, swirling to grease the side of the pan. Pour in half of the egg mixture and sprinkle with half of the cheese strips. Pour in the remaining egg mixture. Reduce the heat to low, cover the frittata, and cook for 15 minutes or just until the bottom is set.

★ BAKE AND SERVE: Transfer the frittata to the oven and bake, uncovered, until the top of the eggs is set. Scatter the remaining cheese strips over and bake 1 more minute. Remove the frittata from the oven and let stand for 4 minutes. Cut the frittata into 6 wedges and serve hot.

NUTRITION INFORMATION PER SERVING — protein: 19 g; fat: 26 g; carbohydrate: 9 g; fiber: 2 g; sodium: 534 mg; cholesterol: 325 mg; calories: 332.

With just a few vegetables to chop and barley that cooks up quickly, this filling soup is the very definition of a week-night dinner in minutes. Pick up whole-grain rolls or buttermilk biscuits on your way home and warm them in the oven while the soup cooks.

Quick Barley and Spring-Vegetable Soup

1 tablespoon vegetable oil

3 medium carrots, peeled and sliced

1 medium onion, thinly sliced

1 large leek, cleaned and sliced crosswise

3 cups coarsely chopped Swiss chard

2 cups sliced fresh button mushrooms

4 cups vegetable broth

3 cups water

1/2 teaspoon salt

1/2 teaspoon ground black pepper

1 cup quick-cooking barley

★ MAKE THE SOUP: In a 6-quart saucepot, heat the oil over medium heat. Add the carrots, onion, and leek; sauté 5 minutes. Add the chard and mushrooms; cook for 1 minute. Add the vegetable broth, water, salt, and pepper and bring to a boil over high heat. Stir in the barley. Reduce the heat to low. Cover the soup and simmer until the barley and vegetables are tender—about 15 minutes.

★ TO SERVE: Divide the soup among serving bowls and serve immediately.

Tip To ensure that all of the sand and grit is released from the leeks, slice to expose the layers, then soak them in a bowl of water, gently opening the layers to remove any trapped debris. Lift the leeks out of the water with a slotted spoon.

NUTRITION INFORMATION PER SERVING – protein: 3 g; fat: 2 g; carbohydrate: 11 g; fiber: 2 g; sodium: 417 mg; cholesterol: 5 mg; calories: 71.

This hearty offering features the sweet, creamy flesh of buttercup squash, a winter variety that has a hard green shell and a turbanlike shape, and the deeply satisfying texture of barley. Serve it with a salad of baby spinach and red onion.

Buttercup-Barley Stew

2 teaspoons cumin seeds

1 tablespoon vegetable oil

1 large onion, chopped (about 1^1/$_2$ cups)

^{1}/$_3$ cup quick-cooking barley

1 teaspoon sugar

2 large cloves garlic, finely chopped

2 tablespoons all-purpose flour

1 tablespoon chili powder

^{1}/$_2$ teaspoon salt

1 2-pound buttercup or other winter
    squash, peeled, seeded, and cut into
    1-inch pieces (about 5^1/$_2$ cups)

2 cups water

1 14^1/$_2$-ounce can vegetable broth

^{1}/$_2$ cup chopped red bell pepper

^{1}/$_4$ cup finely minced fresh cilantro leaves

★ MAKE THE STEW: In a large saucepan, toast the cumin seeds over medium heat until fragrant—about 1 minute. Remove the cumin from the pan and set aside. Add the oil to the saucepan and heat. Add the onion, barley, sugar, and 1 teaspoon toasted cumin seeds and sauté until the onion is lightly browned—about 5 minutes. Stir in the garlic, flour, chili powder, and salt. Add the squash, water, and broth and bring to a boil. Reduce the heat to medium-low, cover, and simmer for 10 minutes. Remove the cover and continue to simmer until the squash is very tender and the stew thickens—about 10 more minutes. Stir in the remaining toasted cumin seeds, the bell pepper, and cilantro. Serve immediately.

NUTRITION INFORMATION PER SERVING — protein: 6.3 g; fat: 6 g; carbohydrate: 46 g; fiber: 10.8 g; sodium: 1,255 mg; cholesterol: 0; calories: 243.

Eggplant and white beans lend such heartiness to this vegetarian combination, you'll never even miss the meat. Chipotle peppers and roasted vegetables add smoky heat.

Chipotle-Vegetable Chili

2 tablespoons olive oil

1 medium onion, sliced

1 pound button mushrooms, quartered

1 small eggplant, cubed

2 medium zucchini, cubed

1 red bell pepper, seeded and diced

2 cloves garlic, minced

1/2 teaspoon salt

1 bay leaf

1 teaspoon chili powder

1 dried chipotle chile pepper, soaked
    1 minute in boiling water, stemmed,
    seeded, and diced

1 19-ounce can cannellini beans, rinsed
    and drained

1 14 1/2-ounce can low-sodium
    vegetable broth

1 14 1/2-ounce can low-sodium
    diced tomatoes

2 tablespoons chopped fresh parsley

★ SAUTÉ THE VEGETABLES: In a large Dutch oven, heat the olive oil over medium-high heat until hot but not smoking. Add the onion and mushrooms. Sauté until the mushrooms soften—about 5 minutes. Add the eggplant, zucchini, and bell pepper. Cook, stirring often, until the vegetables start to soften—about 5 minutes. Add the garlic and cook, stirring often, for 2 more minutes.

★ COOK THE CHILI: Stir in the salt, bay leaf, chili powder, chipotle pepper, cannellini beans, vegetable broth, and tomatoes. Bring to a boil and reduce the heat to low. Simmer, uncovered, for 20 to 30 minutes, until the vegetables are tender and the flavors well blended. Remove and discard the bay leaf.

★ TO SERVE: Stir in the parsley and serve hot.

Tip *Be sure to remove all of the seeds from the chipotle pepper; they are the source of intense heat, which can overwhelm this dish.*

NUTRITION INFORMATION PER SERVING — protein: 7.8 g; fat: 6.1 g; carbohydrate: 29.7 g; fiber: 8.4 g; sodium: 957 mg; cholesterol: 0; calories: 191.

The hot-sweet flavors of the Caribbean islands come together in this allspice-and-cinnamon-infused vegetarian chili. The heat hails from a liberal dose of chili powder and a dash of cayenne, while brown sugar and bananas sweeten the pot.

Blue Mountain Jerk Chili

3 tablespoons chili powder

1 teaspoon ground cumin

1 teaspoon dried oregano

1 teaspoon light brown sugar

$^1/_2$ teaspoon ground allspice

$^1/_2$ teaspoon ground cinnamon

$^1/_2$ teaspoon ground red pepper

1 pound firm tofu, cut into $^1/_2$-inch cubes

2 tablespoons vegetable oil

1 large onion, chopped

3 cloves garlic, minced

1 14$^1/_2$-ounce can low-sodium vegetable broth

1 14$^1/_2$-ounce can low-sodium diced tomatoes

1 ripe banana, mashed

1 tablespoon rum (optional)

1 teaspoon salt

★ SEASON THE TOFU: In a small bowl, mix together the chili powder, cumin, oregano, brown sugar, allspice, cinnamon, and ground red pepper. Sprinkle the tofu with 1 teaspoon of the spice mixture and toss to coat evenly. Reserve the remaining spice mixture.

★ BROWN THE TOFU AND VEGETABLES: In a large Dutch oven, heat the oil over medium-high heat until hot but not smoking. Add the tofu and cook until it begins to brown—about 4 minutes. Add the onion and cook until translucent—about 3 minutes.

★ MAKE THE CHILI: Add the garlic, reserved spice mixture, vegetable broth, and tomatoes to the tofu mixture. Bring to a boil, then reduce the heat to low; simmer, uncovered, for 20 minutes.

★ FINISH THE CHILI: Stir in the banana, rum, if using, and salt. Simmer, uncovered, for 10 more minutes. Serve hot.

NUTRITION INFORMATION PER SERVING — protein: 14.2 g; fat: 12.4 g; carbohydrate: 17 g; fiber: 3.6 g; sodium: 706 mg; cholesterol: 0; calories: 218.

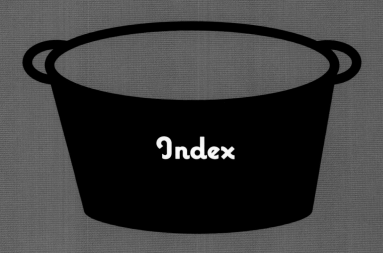

Index

Photography Credits

Page 6: Ann Stratton; **Page 12:** Ann Stratton; **Page 14:** Ann Stratton; **Page 17:** Ann Stratton; **Page 19:** Ericka McConnell; **Page 21:** Judd Pilossof; **Page 22:** Judd Pilossof; **Page 25:** Dennis Gottlieb; **Page 28:** Dennis Gottlieb; **Page 31:** Evan Sklar; **Page 33:** Judd Pilossof; **Page 34:** Judd Pilossof; **Page 36:** Charles Gold; **Page 39:** Ann Stratton; **Page 47:** Judd Pilossof; **Page 49:** Judd Pilossof; **Page 50:** Judd Pilossof; **Page 52:** Dennis Gottlieb; **Page 57:** Ann Stratton; **Page 58:** Ann Stratton; **Page 60:** Ann Stratton; **Page 63:** Alan Richardson; **Page 64:** Louis Wallach; **Page 68:** Louis Wallach; **Page 70:** Louis Wallach; **Page 72:** Louis Wallach; **Page 75:** Alan Richardson; **Page 77:** Judd Pilossof; **Page 78:** Beatriz Da Costa; **Page 80:** Charles Schiller; **Page 84:** Dennis Gottlieb; **Page 87:** Judd Pilossof; **Page 91:** Ann Stratton; **Page 93:** Judd Pilossof; **Page 95:** Charles Gold; **Page 96:** Ann Stratton; **Page 97:** Alan Richardson; **Page 101:** Steven Randazzo; **Page 102:** Alan Richardson; **Page 105:** Judd Pilossof; **Page 106:** Judd Pilossof; **Page 111:** Thayer Allyson Gowdy; **Page 113:** Ann Stratton; **Page 114:** Dennis Gottlieb; **Page 121:** Judd Pilossof